"So often we feel we have to choose between two desirable but apparently opposing objectives when leading organizations. Joel shows us how to be both loving and accountable; to be profitable and caring; to be effective and be giving. He has written *Love Works* as a businessman. But if government and some nonprofits would apply just a fraction of his message in their leadership too, they would be both more effective and happier places."

—*Bill Haslam, Governor of Tennessee*

"Joel and HFE have an outstanding reputation in our industry. Yet what surprised me and delighted me as I read: this is *not* just another book about management. It is about life and love and leadership and how to build prosperity and happiness in your organization ... and yourself. I highly recommend it."

—*Al Weiss, CEO, Weiss Advisors*

"It's one thing to know that 'love is an action,' but far more challenging to make that 'action' a way of life — at work and at home. Reading *Love Works* will transform your life. Drawing on his own experiences, with humility and humor, Joel Manby provides all the tools you'll need to care for others without compromising your desire for excellence. I've known Joel well for over twenty-five years and have never met a leader more qualified to write on this topic."

—*Kevin J. Jenkins, President and Chief Executive Officer,*
World Vision International

"Joel masterfully weaves business principles into stories any leader can appreciate. While he is a CEO, the lessons can apply to any setting — work, home, and even the entertainment world. Joel does not speculate on how something may work or how others succeeded. He tells you how *he* actually did it and recounts his real life path not just to success but to fulfillment as well."

—*Jeff Foxworthy, Entertainer*

"It has been said that real success is about becoming the total person God wants you to be and accomplishing the goals that He helps you set for your life. As leaders, we have a unique opportunity to help others find success by treating them with honor, dignity, and respect and inspiring them to reach higher, dream bigger, strive harder, and go farther than they could ever go on their own. In *Love Works* Joel Manby outlines a proven model for creating and sustaining a successful life and a successful organization by leading ... with love."

—*Dan T. Cathy, President & COO, Chick-fil-A, Inc.*

"I believe this book is the most unique and best-sourced business and management book on the shelf today. I've known Jack and Pete Herschend most of my life. Besides owning the world's number one theme park, the Herschend family has been known for decades as a leader in excellence in the entertainment industry. They live a life of love, and they lead with love. Joel Manby has humbly embraced the timeless principle of leading with love and has expanded HFE nationally with the same value-based leadership style. He has penned an excellent resource for leading with love in the workplace! It will forever change, impact, and improve your company's productivity in immeasurable ways.

—*Joe White, President, Kanakuk Kamps,*
and Founder, Kids Across America

"Joel Manby's compelling new book is a practical road map to compassionate, yet accountable leadership in a troubled world that needs both. I have known Joel for many years and have watched him learn to lead with love and strive to serve with a caring heart at home, work, and church. It is a must read for anyone who leads anybody in the nonprofit or for-profit world."

—*Andy Stanley, Senior Pastor, North Point Ministries*

"I have read a lot of leadership and management books in my thirty-five years as a CEO and in politics. I have never read one as unique and inspiring yet practical as *Love Works*. People in Washington, politics, and government could learn soooo much from this book. Joel is a business executive, but what he teaches us here applies to any organization or leadership or associative endeavor. I dare say that much of the problem in Washington right now is that we are very far away from the principles outlined in this excellent work."

—*John Campbell, Member of Congress, 48th District, California*

"If this book doesn't help and inspire you to be a great leader, I don't know what could. Love works and so does Joel Manby. He is everything this book represents and more. I feel privileged to know him and blessed to be able to work alongside him."

—*Dolly Parton, Entertainer and Herschend Family Entertainment Business Partner*

"In a world where so many think they know what great leadership is all about, Joel has the courage and confidence to speak of leadership in the language of love. Love as a verb. Love as a strategy. Love as a leadership principle—not just at home or at church, but in the rough-and-tumble, results-oriented, hard-charging workplace. Joel's insights and first-hand stories will give you a personal and refreshing look at becoming the kind of leader that people will want to follow."

—*Bonnie Wurzbacher, Senior Vice President, Global Customer & Channel Leadership, The Coca-Cola Company*

"No matter where you are in your journey as a person or a leader, there are great moments of truths and wisdom to inspire you. Joel's transformation is proof that you can make the world a better place, use love as a verb in the workplace, and be profitable all in the same environment."

—*Kim Schaefer, CEO, Great Wolf Resorts Inc.*

"*Love Works* is an amazing book on leadership, written by a very gifted and humble leader, Joel Manby. In this book Joel lays out a clear and compelling case for a leadership model that motivates employees and generates results: Love. Not Love the emotion, but Love the verb. Love as defined in 1 Corinthians 13. I know Joel and his team at Herschend Family Entertainment, and I know that he has driven outstanding results while fully living out the principles he relates in this book. The principles and the stories he shares are powerful, and you will be thoroughly challenged and blessed. I cannot wait to share this book with my team."

—*Charles A. Bengochea, President & CEO, The Original Honey Baked Ham Co. of Georgia, Inc.*

"I wish this book had been written years ago. *Love Works* should be required reading for every aspiring business school student in the country. Not only do the principles work, but they are dynamic, and if implemented on a wide-spread basis, they will help lead to exponential growth in both the top and the bottom line—in business and life!"

—*Tony Cimmarrusti, CEO of Majestic Capital*

"For every leader who has ever wondered what role, if any, compassion has in running a business successfully, *Love Works* provides an inspiring answer. Joel's journey—the ups, the downs, and ultimately the lessons learned—is so compelling that I finished it in a single afternoon. It's a must read for leaders who care."

—*Joe Kennedy, CEO, Pandora*

"*Love Works* delivers an inspirational message that empowers leaders to better engage with their most valuable assets—their people. Joel's ability to interweave his own experiences into the book captivates the reader and provides clear insight into the strength of agape Love."

—*Stefanie Miller, Group Vice President, Strategic Partnership Marketing, The Coca-Cola Company*

"*Love Works* is about life, love, and leadership and how to build prosperity and happiness in your organization ... and yourself. Joel captures the essence of true servant leadership—something we strive to achieve in our business every day. I highly recommend it."

—*Walt Ehmer, President & COO, Waffle House, Inc.*

"Joel Manby is the epitome of a servant leader, one who expects qualities like kindness, patience, and selflessness in his employees while also demonstrating them himself. The seven principles of effective leadership he shares in this book, all of which are based on the Word of God, are truly timeless and echo the simple commandment of Jesus to love others as we would ourselves."

—*Phillip Bowen, CEO, In Touch Ministries*

"I was originally skeptical of the concept of blending 'love' and work. But as I read more, I realized that love coupled with a commitment to performance and accountability really does work! I think all leaders will find *Love Works* balanced, inspiring ... and most importantly, challenging!"

—*Bob Patton, Vice Chairman, Ernst & Young Advisory Services*

"*Love Works* is a lifestyle that Joel lives well. If you want to know how to get results and love people, then you need to consume this book!"

—*Jeremie Kubicek, CEO of GiANT Impact and Best-Selling Author of* Leadership Is Dead

"Having known Joel for many years, I can assure you that he really does live out the practices he espouses in *Love Works*. Joel is someone who not only cares about people but also delivers results, and this book describes with clarity how these two things go hand in hand."

—*Bill Burke, Former President of TBS and The Weather Channel Companies and Co-Author of* Call Me Ted

"*Love Works* is a must read for any leader, whether they lead a company or a family. Practicing the principles of being patient, kind, trusting, unselfish, truthful, forgiving, and dedicated will strengthen your business *and* your family."
— *Warren Jobe, Senior Vice President (Retired), Southern Company*

"Joel Manby represents a unique breed of leader. In *Love Works* he outlines, in practical terms, how to effectively build a great organization and care for people at the same time; he proves that it's not only possible, but crucial for lasting success."
— *Reggie Joiner, CEO & Founder of Orange*

"If you lead a large company, a thriving church, a growing family, an aspiring sports team, or a group of friends — *Love Works* is a must! I am convinced that by following the seven principles in this book you will become successful in whatever leadership role you have."
— *Chuck Tilley, President, Tilley Enterprises, LLC*

"Knowing Joel for over a decade, I have witnessed him leading with these principles firsthand. Whether you are just beginning or well into your career, I highly recommend this informative and enjoyable read as a handbook for successfully combining business and caring leadership."
— *Richard Kinzel, Former President, CEO, & Chairman of the Board of Cedar Fair Entertainment Company*

"*Love Works* captures the culture and business practices that make HFE one of the most productive private companies in the U.S. as well as one of the most fulfilling and nurturing places to work. This book articulates the missing link in corporate America's search for efficiency, profits, and leadership development."
— *Donna F. Tuttle, Former Deputy Secretary of Commerce; Board Director of Herschend Family Entertainment*

"Joel Manby in practice and in this writing represents the best of humanity. In this book Joel provides insights into personal and organizational values that can lead to sustainable high performance by a committed, loyal family of employees. The 'Seven Timeless Principles' and the practical application of them are a foundation for achieving leadership success in our organizations and personal lives. Who would not want to dedicate his or her scarce working hours to such a leader?"

—*John Spiegel, Chairman, Community and Southern Bank, Chairman, S1 Corporation; Retired Vice Chairman & CFO, SunTrust Banks*

"As a global recruiter and advisor of Fortune 500 CEOs, I've read lots of books on leadership. I have found *Love Works* to be a remarkable narrative on how timeless principles can transform an organization. It's a game changer to move leaders beyond Love as a feeling to Love as an action that delivers sustainable business results. Here Love is a critical competence for effective leadership. It surprises many that *Love Works* actually works in the global marketplace of the twenty-first century. The idea may appear to be simple and obvious at first blush, but many leaders miss it and suffer greatly for it. Carpe Diem."

—*Dale E Jones, Vice Chairman, Heidrick & Struggles*

"Joel is the perfect leader for these turbulent times. He trusts his associates to be responsible for their actions, and they trust him to be fair. Best of all, he leads with compassion and love, which gives everyone a sense of purpose. His book is a roadmap to this inspirational leadership."

—*Nelson Schwab, Managing Partner, Carousel Capital*

"After reading *Love Works*, I not only know what Joel thinks about leadership, but also know how to do it. This is the most practical 'how-to' book on organizational leadership I've read."
— *Regi Campbell, Entrepreneur and Author of* Mentor like Jesus *and* About My Father's Business

"*Love Works* is that rare book that offers both inspiration and highly practical advice. Joel Manby and Herschend Family Entertainment demonstrate that leading with love works. If you want to improve your organization and be 'the same person all the time,' don't just read the book—put these lessons into practice."
— *Todd Schurz, President & CEO, Schurz Communications, Inc.*

"Love is not a word heard in many business school classes. But if you read Joel's book, you'll see that leading with love can transform a company's culture. It's about lifting up each other as well as the bottom line. You can have it both ways."
— *Jim Apple, President & CEO, Burroughs & Chapin Company, Inc.*

"Joel Manby is the 'real deal' leader—the boss we all longed to work for. I wish I had read this book early in my career."
— *Rick Woolworth, Former Managing Director, Morgan Stanley*

"Joel Manby's book provides a proven leadership equation first implemented by our Lord Jesus Christ. Joel, through his experiences as President of Saab Automobile USA and now as CEO of Herschend Family Entertainment, has been in situations where these leadership principles have not been the norm and where they have been practiced, and he has had firsthand experience as to which style is effective. One couldn't ask for a better guide promoting a leadership style in the business world today that has had conclusive results as to what works. I highly recommend this book."
— *Diane Paddison, Chief Strategy Officer of Cassidy Turley, Founder of 4Word, and Author of* Work, Love, Pray

LOVE
WORKS.

LOVE WORKS.

SEVEN TIMELESS PRINCIPLES FOR EFFECTIVE LEADERS

JOEL MANBY

ZONDERVAN®

ZONDERVAN.com/
AUTHORTRACKER
follow your favorite authors

ZONDERVAN

Love Works
Copyright © 2012 by Joel K. Manby

This title is also available as a Zondervan ebook.
Visit www.zondervan.com/ebooks.

This title is also available in a Zondervan audio edition.
Visit www.zondervan.fm.

Requests for information should be addressed to:
Zondervan, *Grand Rapids, Michigan 49530*

Library of Congress Cataloging-in-Publication Data

Manby, Joel, 1959-
    Love works : seven timeless principles for effective leaders / Joel Manby.
       p. cm.
    ISBN 978-0-310-33567-2 — ISBN 0-310-33567-1 1. Leadership. 2. Virtues.
I. Title.
HD57.7.M3874 2012
658.4'092 — dc23   2012002571

Published in association with the literary agency of D. C. Jacobson & Associates
LLC, an Author Management Company, www.dcjacobson.com.

Cover design: *Extra Credit Projects*
Author photo: *Dave and Mei's Photography*
Interior photography: *Joel K. Manby*
Interior design: *Matthew Van Zomeren*

Printed in the United States of America

13 14 15 16 17 18 19 /DCI/ 19 18 17 16 15 14 13 12 11 10 9 8 7

To Mom and Dad
for teaching me to love at home

and

Jack and Peter
for teaching me to love at work

Contents

Foreword

June 16, 1998. It was a typical Tuesday morning in Atlanta, Georgia. I had flown into town to meet with a potential board member for the company my brother and I cofounded, Herschend Family Entertainment. But where was he? I glanced at my watch for the fifth time. 9:20 AM. Joel Manby was twenty minutes late. *Twenty* minutes! Clearly I'd made the wrong choice in asking him to be part of the team. I'd been impressed with his credentials and experience, but I'd wondered about his values: would he *get* our company culture?

And would he ever actually show up?

I took a last look at my watch. It seemed like he would be a nonstarter — probably just another hot-shot businessman with a character as shallow as a sheet of paper. That's when Joel walked in — he'd gotten lost in those pre-GPS days — and the rest, as we like to say, is Herschend family history. Today Joel serves HFE as CEO and President, and our company has grown from nine to twenty-six properties located in ten states with exceptional financial results. Joel was *exactly* the right man to lead.

Now don't misunderstand me: I'm *still* not happy Joel was late! I'm extremely punctual, and I expect my team to be punctual as well. But the fact that Joel went from such a rough start to such a strong finish is actually testament to a simple but overlooked idea:

Love works.

You see, when Joel walked in twenty minutes late to that first meeting, I had every right to let that *first* impression be my *last* impression. One strike and he would be out. But I decided to interview him anyway, and it didn't take long for me to realize that giving him a second chance was one of the best decisions I'd ever made. It was the right thing to do.

What I didn't have words for at the time, but what I knew in my bones, is that doing the right thing in business doesn't have to come at the expense of the bottom line. When I gave Joel a second chance, that was forgiveness in action—one of the principles this book discusses—and it absolutely helped our company flourish financially. Wise leaders use their personal ethics to effectively *manage* the tension between corporate values and corporate profits. At the end of the day, that works best for everyone:

Shareholders are glad the company is healthy.

Employees are grateful to work for a company that truly cares about them.

And customers see something special ... and keep coming back for more.

Friend, the book you hold in your hand isn't testament to a single man or a single company. It's much bigger than that. It's about seven principles of effective leadership that have been around for thousands of years but are often forgotten or dismissed. It's engaging and practical. And it's about the best way to lead, a way that will bring bottom-line results and deep contentment.

Love works. Trust me—I see the proof every day that I go to work with Joel.

Sincerely,

Jack Herschend
Cofounder and Chairman Emeritus,
Herschend Family Entertainment

Introduction
Undercover Love

As I fumbled for my alarm at 3:00 a.m. on my first day on the job as a street washer, I wondered what I was getting myself into. The CBS television network had asked my company to participate in its hit reality show *Undercover Boss*. As president and CEO of Herschend Family Entertainment (HFE), I'd agreed to work at Silver Dollar City, our original theme park in Branson, Missouri.

So I stumbled out of bed and put on an unfamiliar uniform: work jeans, black safety boots, a jean jacket layered over a hooded sweatshirt, and false glasses. Thankfully my thirty-five-dollar a night motel room had a coffeemaker, so I sipped the hot brew and tried to remember that I was now officially John Briggs, a laid-off autoworker looking for a fresh start.

The whole project was risky: what if the very act of going "undercover" exposed our workers or our company to ridicule or embarrassment? That would make compelling television for CBS, but it would be unfair to our company. My leadership team at HFE decided to trust our corporate culture and the genuine devotion and goodwill of our hardworking employees. After all, we experienced it firsthand every day, just like the guests at our theme parks, so wouldn't it be wonderful to share that vision with viewers all over the country?

These thoughts were quickly driven from my mind when I arrived at Silver Dollar City at 4:00 a.m. — you don't have a lot of time for introspection when you're being taught to wash streets with a high-pressure hose in the freezing predawn air!

Richard was my mentor, a quiet and humble man who reminded me of my father. At one point, I lost control of the hose and sprayed Richard. The CBS producers may have been secretly hoping for an outburst of anger, but Richard simply looked at me and said in a calm voice, "You might just stay behind me." As we worked, I learned Richard's home had been flooded six months earlier, and he had been forced to move his wife and five children into a pop-up trailer while he scrimped and saved to pay for the renovations. This was a huge strain on both his budget and his family life, yet he always worked with a cheerful attitude.

Later that day, I worked with Albert, a young man who worked as a supervisor at the front gate area at Silver Dollar City. Albert is a sparkplug full of energy and creative ideas to improve the park. He spent some of our time together showing me his roller coaster designs, and he told me that it's his desire to someday be the CEO of the company. As I later struggled with the front gate ticket system, I was wishing he had spent a little more time training me instead! At least the sun had come out and my hands were beginning to thaw from the morning street washing.

As the day wore on, I learned Albert was having tremendous difficulties obtaining college credits because he was trying to squeeze coursework around his full-time job at HFE — and trying to get married soon too! He was working about fifty hours a week, going to school at night, and trying to keep a bride-to-be happy, yet he still had the time and energy to help me, "the new guy," get used to his first day on the job.

I worked with four other people at four other properties that week, but the pattern was the same: hardworking, dedicated employees doing a great job, even while struggling with some aspect of life. They loved the company, they shared the desire to achieve our mission: "make memories worth repeating," and our culture—a culture molded by our founder and purposefully crafted to carry into the future—matched their caring hearts.

At the end of the show, when I revealed my true position at HFE, we rewarded each of these six employees with a grant from our Share It Forward Foundation to address their particular financial need. In chapter 6 you will see how these programs are funded and structured, but seeing them in action so moved me—and the viewers—that for the first time I truly grasped their importance.

Richard was literally stunned, unable to move or speak, as we presented him with a $10,000 check to fix his home so he could move out of his pop-up trailer. When we gave Albert a scholarship to attend college full-time, he cried so hard that I asked for the cameras to stop so he could regain his composure. That's how it was with the other people we provided grants to as well. But they weren't the only ones who were affected by seeing love in action.

Expecting More from Leaders

More than eighteen million viewers saw our episode of *Undercover Boss*, making it the highest-rated program on CBS that week and the second most popular show on any network, trailing only *American Idol*. After the airing, my cell phone seemed like it was ringing 24/7, and page after page of messages filled up our social media accounts on Twitter, Facebook, and email. Our corporate website, for instance, averages fifty hits per day, but in the first forty-five minutes after the show, we got sixty thousand! People who witnessed our employees in action were intrigued by something, and they wanted to know more.

One man from California wanted to let us know what he had seen. "If I didn't already have a job right now—and in this [economy] thank God that I do—I would apply at your company over and over again until I was hired, even if I was picking up trash," he wrote. "I would be so proud to be part of a company like yours."

His sentiment was repeated over and over by people who wanted us to know that they wished their own places of work were more like what they had seen on *Undercover Boss*—in other words, more respectful, cooperative, joyful and, well, more *loving*.

The volume of requests to learn more about our organizational culture and our employee-initiated assistance foundation was overwhelming. I needed to limit my outside engagements for the sake of the business, but a quiet voice inside kept suggesting that this message was exactly what people in all sorts of organizations—businesses, nonprofits, and government agencies—needed to hear.

The simple truth is this: there is a crisis of confidence in leadership. The level of dissatisfaction and even resentment present in the thousands of letters and email messages shocked me. People felt as if they couldn't trust their leaders and bosses. That's why our episode of *Undercover Boss* provoked such an overwhelming response—people were hungry for something new, something better. Countless workers wanted more from their leaders and their work environment, and we were hearing about it.

What's Love Got to Do with It?

The most satisfying part about appearing on *Undercover Boss* was that it confirmed the wise management philosophy that the leaders at HFE had been nurturing for half a century: *leading with love*.

Leading with love is counterintuitive in today's business environment because it turns many so-called leadership principles upside-down. Yet the outpouring of support from people who had never even heard of HFE convinced me that while we might be doing something slightly crazy by leading with love, we were also doing something that people were hungry to be part of.

As I tried to process my experience on the show and the response to it, I was asked to participate in a panel discussion by the Society of Human Resource Managers. While I was on stage, the subject of *Undercover Boss* came up, and what happened next took me by surprise.

When the host asked me what was behind our caring culture displayed on the program, I said, "Well, we actually use love to define our leadership culture at HFE. Not love the emotion, but love the verb. We train our leaders to love each other, knowing that if they create enthusiasm with their employees, the employees will in turn create an enthusiastic guest experience. I think most organizations avoid discussions about how people should treat each other, and I think that's what is wrong with a lot of organizations. Why are we so afraid to talk about love?"

Unexpectedly, the crowd applauded—and kept applauding! Of all the topics covered that night, the discussion about how people treat each other at work and using love in business was the *only* subject that generated strong applause. People were longing to learn more about leading with love.

Soon after that, I gave a keynote talk at our industry convention in Orlando. Over thirty thousand attendees were at this convention from attraction companies all over the world, including Disney, Universal, and hundreds of others.

I spoke to a sold-out lunch crowd about HFE's history and our philosophy of leading with love. Although I touched on our overall business model, I spent most of the time discussing how we used love to define our leadership approach.

The response was encouraging. After my talk, attendees on the convention floor continuously stopped me to express their appreciation for sharing that kind of message. They, too, wondered if leading with love might really be the good news for their organizations that it seemed to be.

The headline in the industry paper the next day featured my speech and the headline: "What's Love Got to Do with It?"

I answered the headline's question in my head: *Everything!*

And that's why you're holding this book in your hands. No matter what kind of organization you're part of, and no matter what level of leadership responsibility you hold, you're reading this because you're hoping that there's a better way to lead than simply "hitting the numbers" and caring only about the bottom line.

I can tell you unequivocally that there is a better way, and that way is leading with love. It's a way to lead that grows the bottom line *and* respects employees, a way to lead that demands accountability *and* gives second chances. In short, it's a powerful way to transform the way you lead and the culture of your organization.

I don't expect you to believe this until you read the stories and principles in this book. My experience isn't a fairy tale. In fact, it's full of pain and false-starts and failures. But I can tell you that coming to HFE changed the way I view leadership and the way I live my life. By the end of this book, I hope I will have convinced you of one thing: *love works*.

1

A HARD
DAY'S NIGHT

It's been a hard day's night, and I've been
working like a dog.
John Lennon and Paul McCartney

1.1

Is This What Life Is All About?

It was a cool June evening in 2000. I was sitting alone in a one-room apartment in northern California, more than three thousand miles from my wife and kids in Atlanta. My place was completely bare inside: no pictures, no personal items, not even a single fake plant to warm the joint up. It was just a place to sleep.

Outside, the steady sheets of rain pouring down were a perfect picture of my life. I was the brand-new leader of an Internet startup called GreenLight.com — and the dot-com bubble had just burst.

That night I had consumed enough wine to dull the sharp edge of the emotional pain and stress that were cutting into me. But what was I going to do, drink more and more each night? I had struggled with short seasons of depression before in my life, but this episode was getting the best of me. I didn't know if I could endure the pain anymore. I had no idea where to turn, and for every raindrop spattering against my window, I had a question running through my mind.

My career was like a high-speed treadmill. After graduating from Harvard Business School in 1985, my wife, Marki, and I moved ten times in fifteen years as I accepted new leadership positions of increasing responsibility and pressure. The constant moving put a tremendous strain on our home life and our four girls.

One of our moves was to the startup of Saturn Corporation, which went from zero to $5 billion in revenue in three years. That job required countless hours of single-minded focus. While at Saturn, I was promoted to CEO of Saab North America. The division was losing money, and my job was to change that. The countless late nights and constant travel continued as a result of the seemingly endless pressure to hit the numbers. And we did— my family sticking with me despite my constant absence, while my team and I helped return the company to the second best year in Saab's North American history.

Unfortunately, there was no such thing as a finish line. I never "made it" or earned a chance to spend more time at home with my family. In 1999, three years into my Saab assignment, Asia and South America were added to my responsibilities. So, just one year before the night I sat alone in that empty apartment in California, I spent more than 250 days on the road, mostly in Asia—and even when I was home, I consistently had 6:00 a.m. phone calls with Sweden and 11:00 p.m. phone calls with the Asian markets.

I was burning out, and so was Marki.

On September 13, 1999, I was in Australia for a Saab distributor meeting and called Marki to catch up. As she started to talk, her voice cracked. "This is the second year in a row you've been away on my birthday. When you're home, which isn't often ..."

I could tell she was struggling to speak.

"When you're home, you're not really *home*."

There was a long pause, and I could tell she was trying to gather herself. "This is not what I signed up for," she finally said. "I thought I could handle this, and I've tried. But this isn't working for our family. You're frustrated. You're not happy, and neither am I. The kids don't really know you. Something needs to change."

The moments of silence that followed seemed like eternity.

Marki was right. Something *did* need to change. Divorce wasn't an option for us, but I knew that if I left her "holding the rock" at home, our marriage would never be all that it was meant to be. I wanted a great marriage, and I wanted to be a good dad. So I asked my boss, the CEO of Saab worldwide, if I could return to "only" being CEO of North American operations, which would cut my travel in half.

He refused.

Have you ever had a moment when a single conversation changes the course of your life irrevocably? It's almost as if time slows down so much that you can see the fork in the road. I was determined to make the right choice — and the right choice was *not* the path that lead to year after year of missed birthdays and kids who were slowly becoming strangers.

I made the difficult choice to leave Saab for what I thought was a better lifestyle and a chance to get my family back on track. I decided to take the CEO position at GreenLight.com, the "car tab" at Amazon.com that let people buy a car with a few mouse clicks. I knew a startup would be tough, but I also knew there would be no international travel, and there was a large financial upside.

So I thought. Then the bubble burst, and it took me with it.

On my *first* week of work at GreenLight.com, the NASDAQ crashed and lost more than a third of its value. We weren't yet generating cash, and what was a three-year cash reserve quickly became a ninety-day cushion. In other words, as an organization, we suddenly had only ninety days to live, not the three years I thought we had when I took the job. At the end of my second week of work, I was laying off three-quarters of our team.

How's that for bad timing?

We took our Atlanta home off the market, delaying my family's relocation, since I would be working 24/7 trying to salvage GreenLight.com. I rented an apartment in California and traveled back to Atlanta only once or twice a month.

The path that I had thought would lead me back home to my family had instead led me to a bare, lonely apartment in California, with rain coming down outside and a sense of hopelessness descending inside. As I sat alone, finishing off my last glass of wine, the questions continued to beat against me:

My entire career I've been so driven ... for what?

The harder I work and the higher I'm promoted, the worse life gets. Is there any hope of balancing my career goals with my family goals?

My self-esteem is tied up in the performance of the companies I run. Do I really want my emotional highs and lows to be based on quarterly profit reports? Is that what life is all about?

If this is what a career in the business world looks like, should I go into a different line of work — one that can unite my skills and my values? But is it right to give up all the experience I've gained?

That night I felt the world closing in around me — and I wanted out. In my darkest moments, I wanted out of life itself. I knew what that would do to my family, however, and I didn't want to be that selfish. But what other options did I have?

My cell phone rang. It was Jack Herschend, chairman of the board of Herschend Family Entertainment Corporation (HFE), one of the largest themed entertainment companies in the world. I had been on the board of HFE for three years and thought very highly of Jack and the company.

"Joel, how are you brother?"

I had no words, only tears, as the emotion poured out. Jack's acute empathy skills had a way of doing that to me. He was always quick to listen, and he cared deeply about people.

As quickly as I could, I gathered myself and explained the situation, revealing some cracks I'd kept hidden for years.

What he said next surprised me:

"Joel, the timing of this phone call may be fortuitous. I'm retiring as chairman next year, and all of us on the board would like you to be the next chairman of HFE. We feel the company needs your leadership strengths and style. Would you consider it?"

I was speechless.

"Joel, I know you're struggling with your family situation, and I think the values and culture of HFE are a perfect fit for you."

Culture? Values? My family? Talking about these things in the context of a prospective job was as unusual as it was welcome.

I was unable to speak. My eyes were again filling with tears, and my throat was closing up. Jack and his family had run HFE for more than four decades. He was asking me to take over a legacy that he and his brother, Peter, had built. Why me? Why now?

And his words were not only about him or the company—they were about my personal life as well. He was worried about my family? That night I was too shocked by his offer to understand the answer to my own question: what kind of leader was this?

As I would learn later, the answer was simple: a man who leads with love.

Leading with Love

My career had left me completely unprepared to meet men like Jack and Peter Herschend. All my life I had been living by the numbers because numbers were all my leaders seemed to care about. If I had any deeper principles, I needed to check them at the company door, because once I was at work, it was all about financial performance.

When I performed well, I was rewarded and respected. When I failed, I felt like I was kicked to the curb. It was that simple. Inside I longed for a better way—a way to unite who I was as a business leader with who I was as a *person*. I wanted to care about the people I worked with and for. I wanted to work somewhere that rejected the false dichotomy between profit and people or profit and principles. I wanted, in short, to be the same person all the time: at work, with my family, at my church, and when I was alone.

But I had been in business long enough to know that was a nearly impossible dream.

As it turned out, that call from Jack set in motion a chain of events that would provide answers to many of my questions. I didn't realize it at the time, but my experience at HFE would revolutionize the way I saw — and see — leadership.

This book was born from the conviction that leading with love is the best way to run an organization.

Any organization.

I understand that this is a controversial claim, but I also now understand — all the way to the core of who I am as a leader and a man — that it is true. Love isn't a feeling, but an action, an action by which leaders and entire organizations can experience almost unimaginable success *and* personal fulfillment.

The Bottom Line

Lest you think all this talk about love is an excuse to avoid the hard truths about leading an organization, let me set your mind at ease.

The bottom line is essential.

If we don't hit our financial goals, we cannot achieve the other objectives we have at HFE, like being a "great place to work for great people." However, we achieve profits by doing the right thing for customers and employees; profits are not an end in themselves. Profits are a product of doing the right thing — over and over again.

During the last seven years at HFE, we have grown operating profit more than 50 percent and have earned over a 14 percent annual return for our owners, clearly beating the large and small cap stock market performance during very difficult times. And we have done that while consciously leading with love. Two of our parks have earned the industry's highest honor for quality: the Applause Award.

Sacrificing values for profits is a flawed choice.

At the same time we've experienced financial success, we've also grown in love—and I mean that in a practical, bottom-line way. Our Share It Forward Foundation was established to help our employees who are in need. Employee donations are matched by company profits and the Herschend family adds an additional gift. We've grown from helping about sixty families per year to over seven hundred families per year in just five years—and that is for an employee-initiated giving program in the midst of difficult economic times!

The bottom line is this: we are more profitable than ever and enjoying leading with love more than ever. By actively using the seven principles of leading with love—to be patient, kind, trustful, unselfish, truthful, forgiving, and dedicated—we are ensuring our business is resilient and profitable and our employees motivated and loyal. We do this because it makes good business sense and it's the right thing to do.

The Dilemma

What about you?

Have you ever wondered if it's possible to maximize profits *and* value relationships?

Is the dissonance between the values you hold at home and the values you adopt at work slowly wearing you down?

Do you ever wonder if your work might change the world for the better?

Have you ever wished that work could just—work?

I have wished all of these things, and my experience at HFE has taught me that they can each become a reality—no matter where you work or what your job title is. All it takes is a desire to do the right thing and a lot of hard work.

Some people think leadership is only about the bottom line. What I have learned is that "only" is the wrong word in that sentence. Leadership is about the bottom line *and...*

and loving the people you work with.

and making your community a better place.

and feeling a sense of satisfaction at the end of every day.

and leading employees who can't imagine working anywhere else.

These things aren't mutually exclusive. In fact, the opposite is true: the bottom line is best served when leaders lead with love. That's the counterintuitive journey I would like to lead you on in the chapters that follow.

If you have read this far, I know you're hungry for something beyond business as usual, so let's get started—and transform the way we lead.

2

THE JEDI MASTERS

Do or do not. There is no try.
Yoda

In Star Wars, aspiring Jedi knights must be trained by a Jedi master. The Jedi master is always wiser and more experienced, so he or she is able to train the young Jedi in the proper way. Jedi masters have a strong understanding of a source of energy called the Force — and they always strive to use the Force for good.

Every organization has its Jedi masters. At Herschend Family Entertainment, ours are Jack and Peter Herschend. Yet all organizations, big or small, lose their Jedi masters and go through other difficult leadership transitions. When Jack and Peter retired, the culture was strong, but it wasn't defined and was at high risk of becoming diluted as we continued to grow with new properties.

We needed to define our culture to teach others *how* to lead with love as Jack and Peter had taught by example.

Keeping a Common Tale from Being a Common Tale

It was at Herschend Family Entertainment's November 2006 board meeting that it finally happened. Jack and Peter Herschend had been on HFE's board since 1960, and this would be their last meeting. Forty-six years is a long time to sit on one board, but for HFE, it was all too brief. From that day forward, Jack and Peter would no longer sit at the table with us, no longer offer their vote, no longer share their voice and vision.

It was a big moment, and some of the board members and family tried to talk Jack and Peter out of it. The brothers had, along with their parents and wives, transformed a guided tour at a single cave in Branson, Missouri, into an enterprise entertaining over sixteen million customers a year and employing over ten thousand employees in twenty-six properties across the United States. They would climb any mountain for their employees, and the employees knew it too—which was why HFE had such a powerful sense of corporate unity and enthusiasm. Jack and Peter embodied a rags to *selfless* riches story, and their generosity was a beacon that attracted and kept the absolute finest employees.

The Farewell

There were tears in the room and plenty of mixed emotions. But Jack and Peter have tremendous wisdom and humility. They knew that what mattered was creating an organization built to last, an organization that would stand the test of time. Jack's departing words confirmed what all of us already knew.

Small in stature with thick gray hair and a strong handshake, Jack stood up slowly, feeling the effects of several hip replacements that stemmed from personally testing one too many of the attractions he helped create. Jack's hands were worn from years of working in the parks, hand-pouring cement steps into the cave, and personally planting thousands of trees throughout Missouri as a dedication to the environment. Jack's every deed and word seemed to have a specific purpose.

"I appreciate the calls for Pete and me to stay on the board, but we will not. As you are aware, Pete and I have carefully constructed a ten-year transition. A plan that took me from CEO to chair, chair to voting board member, voting board member to nonvoting board member, and then off the board. Pete is following a similar path. This plan is critical so that the company can transition smoothly while Pete and I are still healthy."

The room was silent; we could have heard a pin drop.

He continued: "It's a common tale for a family business to lose its way after the godfathers leave, which is why Pete and I feel strongly about this. We both understand that in order to keep this special company special, we need to let a new team of leaders and an independent board carry on, out from under our shadow. We want to remain family owned forever, and we want it to feel like a family, but we also want to be led by the best team possible. With this in mind, it's important that the board and the leadership never lose sight of the three main Herschend family objectives: a specified growth in profit so it is 'a great long-term investment,' to be a 'great place to work for great people,' and to 'lead with love.'"

Jack cleared his throat and sipped a glass of water before continuing: "We understand that sometimes tension can exist between these objectives, but that is a tension that needs to be managed. It's not okay to achieve profit growth and destroy our culture as a 'great place to work for great people.' It is also not okay to focus on being a 'great place to work' without achieving our financial objectives. This is a tension to *embrace*, not eliminate. I have great faith in this board and in this leadership team. The time is right."

With that he sat down.

Jack was right. Typically organizations start small with an entrepreneur and/or inspirational founder; they have a caring family-type culture with a workforce completely committed to a cause. However, when these same organizations find themselves in a transition, the founding culture rarely remains intact. For the culture to survive, it must be defined *and* adhered to or the organization could lose its way. Once an organization loses its soul, the financial performance usually starts to decline and the best people leave.

Either that, or it isn't an organization anyone *really* wants to work for.

HFE was committed to avoid becoming another "common tale." We wanted to ensure our special culture thrived as the founders retired and we continued to add properties in other geographic locations. However, we needed to lead with love—just as Jack and Peter had for decades—in a way that could be taught and measured.

Has your organization gone through a similar leadership transition? If not, it will eventually. I believe you will be better positioned if you can identify and maintain a strong culture built on timeless values that drives healthy behavior and achieves strong financial results.

It's to those seven timeless values that we will turn in chapters 3 through 9, but first a brief word about leading with *love*. What is love, anyway?

2.2

Love Is a Verb

I could accept the fact that Herschend Family Entertainment employees loved working for the Herschends, and even that the Herschends loved them back—though that was a bit of a tougher sell, given many of the people I had worked for. But I was struggling with the word *love* and how to define it in a way the employees would understand and accept.

That's when I remembered a talk I'd heard many years before, and the secret I was looking for started to reveal itself.

It was a beautiful day on July 5, 1986, my twenty-seventh birthday. It was also my wedding day, and I was standing at the altar with my beautiful bride, Marki. We were like most newlyweds, of course—all goo-goo eyed for each other, unable to imagine anything but marital bliss. Yet our pastor, Terry Walker, had other thoughts for his talk that day.

Love the *verb*.

Terry told us, "You can't imagine this today, but there will come a day when you are frustrated with each other; you may not feel like you love each other. You may not even feel like you *like* each other in the moment. Joel and Marki, that's when you need to *behave* like you love each other."

More Than a Feeling

Treating someone with love regardless of how you feel about that person is a very powerful principle. This type of love is the basis for all healthy relationships, bringing out the best in ourselves and others. It can make us great spouses, great parents, and great friends.

Great leaders too.

All too often, however, when we read the word *love*, we automatically think about romantic love—the emotional kind.

What I'm talking about, however, is love the *verb*, not the emotion. I'm talking about actions, not feelings. I'm referring to a set of behaviors that people use to build a healthy relationship with someone regardless of how they feel.

Why the communication problem? Because the English language has only one word for love. For purposes of this chapter, it would be better if we all were Greek! The Greek language is more articulate in expressing the distinctions among various types of love. In fact, the ancient Greeks distinguished *four* primary kinds of love: *eros, philos, storge,* and *agape*.

Eros is the love expressed when your teenage daughter bursts through the door and declares, "I'm in love!" As an overly protective father of four beautiful young women, I'm not thrilled with that announcement! *Eros* yielded the English word *erotic*, and it's all about desire, attraction, and warm, fuzzy feelings. This is the romantic love Hollywood has exploited to make billions of dollars.

Sadly, it doesn't stand up very well to pressure. The problem with eros is that it depends on circumstances. If the evening is romantic—if the sunset is gorgeous and the wind warm and ... well, you get the idea—eros can exist. However, as soon as there are hurtful actions or mean words, eros withers. Therefore, eros isn't a reliable basis for building a meaningful or healthy relationship over time—and it's not the foundation on which to build an organization either.

Friends and Family

Most of us recognize *philos* as the root of Philadelphia, the city of brotherly love. Those of us who know Philadelphia Eagles fans may take issue with the "brotherly love" part—after all, these are the fans who booed Santa Claus during halftime! However, this is the word our Greek friends used to describe the love of friendship and the fellowship of being with people we enjoy. *Philos* describes the people you want to hang out with and who want to hang with you too.

Although philos is great, and I *do* know Eagles fans I like, philos can be conditional or even selfish. If you wrong someone, philos can fade; time and distance can end it too. Unfortunately, all of us have lost a philos friendship over one or the other of these circumstances.

Storge, the third kind of love, is the natural affection felt between family members. This is where the term "blood is thicker than water" comes from. A mother's affection for her children compares to no other. Family affection has an exclusivity and acceptance not experienced in philos or eros. Anyone who has lived through parenting a two-year-old tyrant or a teenager knows plenty about storge love!

Philos and storge are still insufficient types of love on which to build an organization, however—we can't always work with our friends or family, right?

Love the Verb

The fourth kind of love, *agape*, is unconditional. It is a decision, a matter of will. Its verb form is *agapao*, but for simplicity I will use *agape* because it's all Greek to me. The key principle is to think of agape as a *verb*, not an emotion.

Agape love is the foundation for the best and noblest relationships that humans are capable of. It is deliberate and unconditional love that is the result of choices and behaviors rather than feelings and emotions.

In that regard, agape love is about the values we embrace as a way of life, and it is a determination to *behave* in a certain way that stems from our regard for other human beings, regardless of how we may feel about them. For leaders, demonstrating agape love is about behavior, not emotion.

This is a critical distinction that explains why agape love can be the motivating force of a successful organization.

Agape love can exist in the most hostile environments — even work! Eros and philos would evaporate in a stress-filled work environment, but agape can stand the test of time. In fact, with agape love, you can dislike someone or be frustrated with them and still treat them with love. Agape love will promote healthy relationships among employees and their leaders, allowing people to perform at their very best, all the while withstanding the pressure and tension that can exist in a high-performance organization.

Those Greeks were onto something!

Agape Love Works

If agape love builds healthy relationships in all walks of life, why shouldn't we always use it to build our organizations as well? Why isn't there more dialogue about how to create and maintain healthy relationships at work? After all, common sense tells us that people will perform better if they are treated with respect and trust.

I have served in large and small organizations, public and private, and also on boards of several nonprofit and for-profit organizations. After more than thirty years of witnessing all forms of organizational structures, I am still surprised at how willingly we discuss strategy and how to increase profit but how loath we are to discuss how to build and maintain a successful corporate culture by consistently treating all employees in a way that attracts and keeps the best talent in all levels of the organization.

That is why I submit that we should never leave love at the door when we come to work. On the contrary, *love works*.

Think about love the verb, not love the emotion. Think agape, not eros, or even philos or storge. Think commitment and will, not feelings, and you will start to see how love works.

Basing the leadership behavior of an organization on the definition of agape love may strike you as a new or even revolutionary idea—and in the context of modern American organization practices, it is. But the inspiration for using agape love as a leadership principle actually comes from one of the oldest and most respected authorities on human behavior in the world: the Bible.

The seven principles we will explore in the rest of this book are paraphrases from 1 Corinthians, a letter written two thousand years ago. Chapter 13 of 1 Corinthians is known as the "love chapter" because there the apostle Paul wrote: "Love is patient, love is kind. It does not envy, it does not boast, it is not proud. It does not dishonor others, it is not self-seeking, it is not easily angered, it keeps no record of wrongs. Love does not delight in evil but rejoices with the truth. It always protects, always trusts, always hopes, always perseveres" (1 Cor. 13:4–7).

This is agape—and these are principles that will transform your organization, from the bottom line to the bottom of your employees' hearts. Love is . . .

- patient
- kind
- trusting
- unselfish
- truthful
- forgiving
- dedicated

How these words get worked out in the context of a successful organization may surprise you—remember, they are *never* an excuse to ignore poor performance or neglect the bottom line.

As you will see in the chapters that follow, agape love is a leadership principle that holds leaders accountable and helps any organization become healthier and more enthusiastic.

Join me as we learn how.

3

PATIENT
HAVE SELF-CONTROL IN DIFFICULT SITUATIONS

You don't have to make headlines to make a difference.

Truett Cathy

The famous chapter in the Bible about love that is often read at weddings — 1 Corinthians 13 — defines love, beginning with an attribute we sometimes forget: "Love is patient."

Patience is mentioned first for a reason. As an attribute of human character, patience is generally underappreciated and undervalued. In a world that has become faster paced than anyone could have imagined even a quarter century ago, exercising patience is honorable — whether it's in line at a fast-food restaurant or while reacting to a bad quarter posted by a direct report.

In the context of leading with love, embracing patience is not about ignoring poor performance. Ever. No experienced leader would tolerate that. When leading with love, the principle of patience means behaving with self-control in difficult situations.

- How can a patient leader survive — and thrive — in a fast-paced organization?
- Are there ways to admonish poor performance while protecting a person's dignity?
- Is there a laser-focused way to use praise to maximum benefit and balance our admonishment?

3.1

Sweden on an Easter Sunday

was still asleep early on Easter Sunday 1999 when my cell phone jolted me awake. It was my boss, the CEO of Saab Worldwide, calling from Trollhatten, Sweden — and even my wife could tell from the way I held the phone an inch away from my ear that he wasn't calling to wish me a pleasant holiday! He was so angry with our sales numbers that he wanted me to fly to Trollhatten that very evening for a "discussion." That meant a red-eye flight with a meeting on Monday at 3:00 a.m. Eastern Time — not exactly what I had been picturing for my Easter day.

Three years earlier I had been promoted to president and CEO of Saab North America. My prior contribution to the successful startup of Saturn Corporation helped me land this position at the age of thirty-six. Saturn was known for excellent marketing and outstanding dealer relationships, both of which were attributes Saab lacked. At the time, General Motors owned half of Saab, so I was moved from Saturn to Saab in order to bring a new direction in leadership.

With the cooperation of a strong team around me, Saab North America soon turned the corner, flipping from a loss of $50 million in 1995 to a profit of $10 million two years later. My team and I had made some tough decisions about vehicle models, marketing, dealer count, and personnel, but we were headed in the right direction.

However, in the first quarter of 1999, product shortages and shipping issues dented our sales, and we missed our numbers by 20 percent. I knew the problem was an anomaly and not representative of the positive direction our North American operation was moving. As the most senior executive on the continent, I didn't have to worry about an angry boss storming into my office and demanding to know why I hadn't met my numbers.

Instead, he summoned me to *his* continent.

As I threw some clothes and toiletries into my carry-on bag, anger and incredulity began to rise inside me. I could scarcely believe I was being forced to drop everything and fly to Sweden — especially when doing so would do *nothing* to boost our sales performance for the next month. We needed the right cars in stock, and we needed time to solve a few production and shipping issues.

When I arrived in Sweden, I felt like a naughty schoolboy being called to the principal's office. They expected me to take my punishment on the very public stage of our global corporate headquarters. In front of my counterparts from around the world, as well as top management in Sweden, our CFO trashed my single quarter of missed sales targets. He was a brash American who seemed to relish the opportunity to let me know exactly how worthless I was for letting the numbers slip in such a critical year for Saab. There was no talk of causes or solutions, just accusation and belittling commentary.

Had my company really just spent $10,000 in airfare to fly me across the Atlantic Ocean for *this*? I was utterly humiliated. As I sat stone-faced in that boardroom, I asked myself, "Five of the last six quarters we've set sales records, and this is the treatment we deserve?"

The urge to shoot back a few choice comments about supply

shortages and manufacturing was almost irresistible. Somehow I mustered enough patience to respond in a controlled manner, showing him more respect than I felt he deserved at the moment. Or perhaps it was my serious case of jet lag that kept me calm! Either way, I was grateful the situation didn't escalate, and before long it was time for me to catch my flight back home.

In the years since that public flagellation, the particulars of what was said and why—as well as my feelings of defensiveness and anger—have melted away. Yet there is one unforgettable aspect of that experience that changed my leadership style for good: from that moment forward, I determined never to publicly admonish people in a way that would diminish their dignity.

Patient Admonishment

That incident marked the beginning of my emotional disconnect from Saab, and within a year I made the ill-fated move to Greenlight.com in an attempt to improve my family life. Yet I'm grateful for the time I was given to serve there, especially because it taught me vital lessons about how to lead with patience without sacrificing performance or accountability.

We all need to be held accountable, and as leaders we are responsible to hold others accountable. However, whenever possible a reprimand should be given in private, and it should be given in a way that maintains a person's dignity. When we admonish our employees in private and in a patient, respectful manner, we go a long way toward ensuring our employees remain motivated and continue to grow. Just imagine what would have happened if my boss at Saab had calmly asked me over the phone to explain my sales numbers. Instead, the public spectacle he insisted on virtually guaranteed that I would miss any corrective lessons that I *did* need to draw from that experience.

Certainly there are times when private admonishment is not the right course of action for a leader, but even then we must remain patient and respectful. For example, just before the last week of the season, the operators at one of our HFE parks suddenly reduced their bottom-line annual forecast by about 20 percent. I knew this reduction had nothing to do with their particular market but instead was a sign that their financial manager was struggling to keep up.

That park had lost track of expenses due to inexperience. About three-quarters of the management team was relatively new, and by the end of the season, the growing number of balls they had been trying to juggle were beginning to come crashing down.

A few weeks later, when we began reviewing our proposed budgets for the upcoming season, I knew I had to hold these managers accountable, but I was still deciding the best way to accomplish that.

As our regular meeting progressed, it became apparent this management team was hoping to fly under the radar and avoid being accountable for their mistake. It was then I decided a public rebuke would be more effective than private admonishment, since they had attempted to gloss over their error.

I looked at that team and said, "We're not moving on yet." After clearly pointing out their year-end shortfall and explaining its causes, I continued. "You all contributed to this problem, and late misses in forecasts like this are unacceptable. This can never, ever happen again. Is that clear?"

At this point, you may be wondering, *what's the difference between this and what your boss at Saab did to you, Joel?* That's a question I've asked myself, and I believe I have an answer.

In the moment, I spoke as calmly and professionally as I could, and I kept my focus on why the shortfall had happened and what could be done to keep it from happening again. I even concluded by encouraging that management team — adding to their emotional bank accounts, which is something we will look at more in the following chapters. I told them I knew they were capable of more, and that I believed they would succeed the following year. I told them I trusted them.

Then, about a year later, when I was having lunch with the general manager from that same park, I received confirmation that my public admonishment had been delivered with respect and love. As we ate burgers and fries on a shady bench in the park, he looked at me and said, "We haven't forgotten. My team had never seen you so stern—and it was good for us."

As business leaders, we can never forget the necessity of admonishing. Leading with love is not an excuse to be "soft" on people. Yet at the same time, we must *always* admonish with patience and respect. Our goal isn't simply performance; it's to protect the dignity of the people on our team. Whether we correct and train our employees in public or in private, our goal is always to do so with respect and love. After all, that's exactly how *we* want to be treated.

At Saab the admonishment I received was simply destructive, like gasoline poured on a tree. What I've learned from Jack and Peter is that the best admonishment is constructive, like the way a patient gardener prunes and waters a tree. Everything he does is with the hope of a better harvest. Handling difficult situations with patient admonishment is a sure sign of leading with love.

3.2

Patient Praise

Praise versus Clichés

Just as leading with love requires patient admonishment, it also requires patient *praise*. Too often praise is an afterthought, merely a nice-sounding cliché — *You know, you've been doing some great work around here* — that we say as a preface to a very specific criticism!

However, for praise to be effective, it needs to be delivered by a leader who is patient enough to observe what his or her team has actually been doing and waits for the right moment to deliver that assessment.

If you don't quite believe me, consider the NCAA's 2011 March Madness basketball tournament. Remember the championship game between Butler and UConn? The one where UConn gave Butler a 53 – 41 drubbing in the worst final in recent memory, where Butler made a mind-bogglingly bad 19 percent of their field goal attempts?

After the game, the head of the tournament selection committee said, "It was a great game."

This public praise about the merit of the game had zero credibility. The same is true when leaders make generalizations like

"Great job" or "You're the best" or "I couldn't have done it without you." It takes patience to praise with specifics, and praise without specifics can be worse than no praise at all.

The Power of Real Praise

It was a brisk and beautiful April day, but I was as nervous as I'd ever been. This was my first day on the job as the new chairman of Herschend Family Entertainment, and Jack Herschend was going to introduce me to some of the key leaders at Silver Dollar City whom I didn't yet know.

There's nothing unusual about feeling nervous about one's first day on the job, but my agitation went *way* beyond usual. I knew that HFE was a family company in every sense of the word, and Jack had been chairman of the company for more than four decades. Now he was getting ready to pass the baton to me—and if he was an Olympic champion, I felt like an uncoordinated fifth grader!

Replacing Jack was the business equivalent of leading the UCLA basketball team the first year after John Wooden retired as the most successful college basketball coach of all time, or going on-air the afternoon after Oprah's final day as host of her talk show. Jack Herschend is a legend in our industry, and as I walked around the park with him, it wasn't the thought of the cotton candy or a roller coaster that was making my stomach do front-flips.

I wondered whether my expertise in the automotive industry would apply in this new arena. I knew that I was about to undergo a huge test of my leadership principles and beliefs— would my convictions and talents be sufficient for this task?

What made things worse was the knowledge that even as I was battling these thoughts, people at HFE were probably thinking, *Wait,* this *is Jack's replacement? All he knows about are cars, and he looks like he's about thirty-five years old!* Anticipating such thoughts, I felt flushed, and my heart began to race.

As we walked the grounds of Silver Dollar City, everyone said hi to Jack. And that's what they all called him too — Jack. Not Mr. Herschend, not sir, not boss — just Jack. Jack stopped to say hello to anyone who wanted to talk. He asked the employees about their families, whom he knew by name. He remembered specific details about whose kids were in college or whose family member was sick. The evidence of his love and affection for his employees was overwhelming. All I could think about was how hard it was for me to remember people's names. I thought, *I will never be as good as Jack. Why am I doing this?*

So what *did* happen that April Day? Did touring the park with Jack and chatting with the friendly employees set my mind and heart at ease?

Not exactly.

We ended our tour, and I was introduced to Nancy, Jack's longtime executive assistant. Her last name wasn't Herschend, but she was like a member of the family and had been Jack's loyal assistant for many years. When Nancy met me, she did her best to smile and be relaxed, but I could tell she was nervous or at least unsettled. We sat in Jack's office and made small talk about our backgrounds and families.

However, as we began to talk about her responsibilities, Nancy's lower lip started to tremble and her eyes welled up with tears — not because of me, but because the fact of Jack stepping down was becoming real for her. I understood intellectually that Nancy wasn't reacting to me per se, but my fears were reinforced, and I began to wonder if my self-doubt was going to be a permanent fixture of my new job.

I started compiling a mental list of auto companies who might hire me.

Leaving Nancy's office, Jack introduced me to Mike Hutcherson and his team. Mike was the leader of all the HFE parks in Branson, Missouri. In other words, Mike and his team were devoted to Jack — and they knew a whole lot more about my job than I did!

That's when Jack changed everything.

In front of Mike and everyone present in the room, Jack began to praise me. He communicated his unwavering support for me, saying, "The most important thing to me about Joel is his values. His beliefs and leadership style are exactly in line with what we want as the chairman of this company. He understands our culture and wants to protect and grow it. There was nobody else I considered for this responsibility. Joel was my first choice. I *know* that he is God's man for the job."

The sense of relief and gratefulness that filled me felt like stumbling into a warm cabin after wandering for hours in the snowy woods.

Jack had never said most of those things to me individually, and certainly never in the form of a praise-filled monologue in a room of influential leaders. His words lifted my spirits and boosted my confidence. A huge weight lifted from my shoulders.

The picture had changed. Jack hadn't run the good race only to watch me fumble the baton as the crowd gasped. Instead, Jack and the HFE crowd had chosen me and were rooting for me. Jack was going out of his way to let everyone know I was his first choice, his only choice, and I had his full support. This gracious exercise made me even more determined to do a good job for Jack, the Herschend family, the board, and the employees.

Getting to the Point

Perhaps praise doesn't require the same level of patience that successful admonishment does. Yet when we rush to praise without thinking, we often fail to praise the right way and we miss an opportunity.

Looking back, I know Jack thought deeply about how to ensure the transition between his leadership and mine was successful. In other words, he was patient enough to wait for the right moment to praise me and patient enough to choose the right words.

It's a good thing Jack wasn't like that NCAA official who praised the UConn-Butler game as being "great." I shudder to imagine what the consequences could have been for my transition if Jack had taken the easy way out and used such dull, impatient praise or failed to walk with me around the park and choose the right moment to publicly praise.

I know Joel is the right guy. He's got what it takes. He's going to bring a lot of great ideas to the table, and I'm excited to see what he's got for us.

It would have been all downhill from there.

To be truly effective, praise must be legitimate and pointed. Will everyone have good reason to believe this praise is true? What exactly is the praise for? In other words, I can walk around town with a megaphone, praising my employees at the top of my lungs, but if what I say isn't believable and specific, it won't have the effect I want.

Jack and Peter have also taught us the value of *balancing* praise with admonishment. They both try to give more praise than admonishment to keep a positive balance in our emotional bank accounts. This is not a science, but I would guess they praise about three times more than they admonish. You always leave a conversation with them feeling positive even if they have asked for improvement.

Have you ever been in a situation when someone complimented you in public for a specific achievement or quality, when that person took the trouble to describe exactly the reason or reasons that you were praiseworthy?

Think about that moment. Remember how you felt. I would bet loyalty to the person giving the compliment welled up inside of you. I would bet you made a commitment not to let that person down in your job performance.

That's exactly how others feel when you praise them with the right words delivered at the right time. Public praise, just as Jack's did for me, empowers your team to be the leaders you already know they are. That's using patience to lead with love.

3.3

A Lesson
from History

We will end our look at patience with a quick trip back in
time to the Civil War—or at least to my favorite movie
about it, the 1993 epic *Gettysburg*.

Following the first day's battle, a meeting takes place between
General Robert E. Lee (played memorably by Martin Sheen) who
commanded the armies of the South and Major General J.E.B.
Stuart (played by Joseph Fuqua) who was in charge of the rebel
cavalry. Union forces had gotten the better of Lee's men in a
bloody way, and a big part of the reason was that General Stuart
provided his boss with inadequate intelligence about the enemy's
positions and movements.

Perfect time for some public admonishment, right? And certainly no praise after how badly Stuart had screwed up!

Lee confronts Stuart in his tent; the private space is lit only by
candles. "It is the opinion of some excellent officers that you have
let us all down," says General Lee.

"General Stuart, your mission was to free this army from the
enemy cavalry and to report any movement by the enemy's main
body. That mission was not fulfilled. You left here with no word
of your movement or the movement of the enemy for several days.

Meanwhile we were engaged here, drawn into battle without adequate knowledge of the enemy's strength or position, without knowledge of the ground. Sir, it is only by God's grace that we did not meet disaster here...."

Lee continues, with passion and conviction but without malice. "Perhaps I did not make myself clear. Well sir, this must be made very clear.... You sir, with your cavalry, are the eyes of this army, and without your cavalry, we are made blind. That has already happened once; it must never, ever happen again."

So far Lee is within his rights as a leader. In fact, we would think him remiss if he didn't call out Stuart for such a grievous failure of intelligence. But what happens next shows the sort of long-range leadership vision that we must have if we are to lead our organizations successfully through changing seasons and challenges.

Stuart begins to offer to resign his post, but Lee cuts him off. "There is no time for that! There is no time!"

Then Lee walks over and puts his hands on Stuart's shoulders.

"There is another fight coming tomorrow, and we need you. You must take what I have told you and learn from it, as a man does."

All has been said about Stuart's performance that needs to be said. Lee concludes, "There has been a mistake. It will not happen again. I know your quality; you are one of the finest cavalry officers I have ever known. Your service to this army here has been invaluable. Now ... let us speak no more of this. The matter is concluded.... Good night, General."

Lee gives Stuart a crisp salute and turns away.

This scene epitomizes the role patience plays in leading with love. Lee could have done many things with Stuart: cursed him, confronted him in the middle of the camp, minimized his skills and talents, and so on. Instead, the way Lee handled his wayward protégé is a model for how every leader should approach criticism:

- Admonish in private whenever possible.
- Be stern but avoid malice.
- Be specific.
- Get people "back on the horse" with pointed praise.
- Move on without a grudge.

Isn't this how all of us want to be treated? Leading with patient love means admonishing privately and praising specifically, and never doing the former without the latter.

How will you lead tomorrow? Whose performance needs to improve this week? Who needs specific praise? Patiently leading with love doesn't mean *waiting* to stop poor performance or bad behavior—it means starting now—but it always means handling tough situations with respect and care.

Patient
Chapter Summary

☑ Patient: have self-control in difficult situations.
  - Don't be patient with poor performance. Be patient with how you *respond* to poor performance.

☑ Praise patiently in public.
  - Be specific and exact.
  - Be legitimate — false praise kills credibility.

☑ Admonish in private.
  - Private admonishment is effective and protects a person's dignity.
  - Get to the point and be specific; reaffirm the person's value; get the person "back on the horse"; and don't speak of the reason for admonishment again.

☑ Praise more than you admonish — think in terms of a 3 to 1 ratio.

4

KIND
SHOW ENCOURAGEMENT
AND ENTHUSIASM

*Anyone who consistently makes you feel
bad is not helping you be better.*
                                    Sam Horn

"How many of you feel like you've had too much encouragement in your life?"

I often ask this question in our Lead with Love leadership training class at HFE, and no one ever raises a hand. Everyday life delivers so many challenges that encouragement is always in short supply. A person cannot be encouraged too much.

Expressing kindness is one important way a leader can help employees overcome life's challenges. Kindness doesn't mean being *nice* all the time; leaders must hold people accountable. However, kindness does mean that encouraging and leading are two sides of the same coin and that words of affirmation and support can be infectiously effective.

- Do you feel too busy and stressed yourself to encourage others?
- Are you afraid people may take advantage of your encouraging leadership style?
- Would you like to learn how to encourage while still driving better performance?

4.1

The Football Banquet

I was a senior, striding the hallways of Battle Creek Lakeview High School on the way to a football banquet. I don't remember the words my football coach spoke at the banquet that night, but I'll never forget the lesson I learned about kindness from my first coach: my mom.

Sports were huge for me. I played football in the fall and basketball in the winter, and ran track and played baseball simultaneously in the spring. My high school was large, and it was common for the stands to be full for games. If you're an athlete on the field, there are lots of people watching *you* from the stands, but you shouldn't be expected to know all of *them*, right?

That's not how Mom saw it. As we turned the corner toward the banquet room that evening, we passed three younger boys who were obviously freshmen. They smiled at us and chorused, "Hi, Joel." I gave them a vague head nod as we walked past, continuing my conversation with my mother.

Wrong move.

As soon as she could steer me into a private space, my mother jabbed her finger into my chest and admonished me.

"You listen to me, young man," she said. "Every time you walk

My first "kindness" coaches: Mom and Dad.

past someone, you have an opportunity to make their day better or make their day worse. And I don't think you made their day better! Those boys clearly look up to you, and because of who you are in this school, you have an opportunity—no, an *obligation*—to try to make their day better, and certainly not to make it worse."

I was stunned.

Mom almost never got upset—and this was certainly the first time she had ever poked her finger in my chest! As the banquet progressed, I collected myself, and while my football coach recapped our season, my mind drifted to what Mom had told me.

I took her message—"make their day better"—to heart. It was strong advice, and it has continued to resonate for my lifetime. Ever since that high school banquet, I have strived to follow her prescription. At the very least, I try to genuinely acknowledge people when I walk past them—no halfhearted head nodding! When I am at my best, I try to make some kind of deposit—even if only a small one—into that person's emotional bank account.

All of us have worked with leaders who are frequently negative and drain their teams. This is especially prevalent during times that are difficult financially or personally. Yet those are the times kindness is more needed than ever!

At Herschend Family Entertainment we try to model the

"make their day better" principle every day and in every interaction. Making someone's day better is contagious and increases the energy, effectiveness, and productivity in any organization. Even when leaders feel concern for what lies ahead, we must give off positive impressions and encouragement if we want our teams to thrive.

Did you miss an opportunity today to make someone's day better? Don't miss that opportunity again. That's leading with love.

4.2

"Spring Hill or Bust"

June 23, 1994, was a hot, rainy day in Spring Hill, Tennessee. The scene looked like something from the movie *Field of Dreams* when hundreds of cars were lined up on the gravel road to see the baseball field Kevin Costner's character had carved from an Iowa cornfield. "If you build it, they will come."

But this scene was even bigger: more than twenty-five thousand cars were lined up for mile after mile, all heading toward an automotive plant. Most of the cars had orange foam balls stuck on their antennas that said "Spring Hill or Bust." Total strangers had driven from all across the country, drawn together by a common purpose. As they arrived and parked their cars, they began to hug, give high-fives, and tell each other stories.

The crazy thing was that they weren't celebrating a rock star or praising a presidential candidate. They were that excited about ... their cars. And not some elite or expensive automotive brand like Mercedes-Benz or BMW, either. No, this was the scene at the Saturn Homecoming, an owner's event that attracted more than forty-three thousand Saturn owners who journeyed to Spring Hill to tour the plant, listen to country-western concerts, and have lots of good old-fashioned fun.

The first Saturn vehicles were simple and practical. There were no supercharged engines to incite the driving enthusiasts, no gizmos in the dashboard to excite techno freaks. What inspired these owners was the way they were treated when they bought or serviced their car. The Saturn Homecoming was simply the chance for Saturn drivers to share the enthusiasm of owning a Saturn with other people who felt the same.

In November 1983, General Motors (GM) announced a new operating unit, the Saturn Corporation. It would be the first new brand since Chevrolet in 1918. Its much-publicized mission was to manufacture a smaller car that could compete with the Japanese. As smaller cars were widely believed to be the future of the industry, GM understood the importance of being able to produce them competitively.

From the start, GM leaders recognized that transforming the experience of purchasing a car could be one key to success for Saturn. Even if GM couldn't clearly beat the Japanese in quality or price, it hoped to make the way Saturns were sold and serviced irresistibly appealing. And considering how painful the car-buying experience was to so many Americans, Saturn was onto something.

Launching with Love

It was an exciting time to work at Saturn. Our brand was tagged, "A Different Kind of Company. A Different Kind of Car." With a "no-hassle, no-haggle" approach at our dealerships, we were coming to market with a revolutionary approach. We planned to require new Saturn dealers to sell cars for the price the dealer marked on the window sticker, to give the customer one fair price for the trade-in vehicle, and to provide one fair interest rate on a loan. No back-and-forth negotiating—and the salespeople were to treat customers with trust and respect, just as they would want to be treated.

We carefully recruited 250 dealers who understood the vision and wanted to treat their customers the right way and change Americans' negative perceptions of the car-buying experience. They embraced Saturn's vision and were passionate about it.

I will never forget the speech Skip LeFauve, the CEO of Saturn, gave to all the employees and dealers. He said, "Loyalty today is no longer a function of rote or duty, but rather passion. You must do things so astonishingly well that customers become not merely loyalists, but rather outright apostles."

LeFauve went on to say, "We want to change the poor reputation of the car-buying process. No more cheating the customer, no more dishonest tactics, no more wheeling and dealing. I want you all to treat the customer as if it was your *own mother* buying the car!"

I had never heard talk like that at GM. Treat the customer like I treated my own mother? Wow—I *loved* my mother! LeFauve's message deeply affected me. Saturn employees and dealers were actually enthusiastic about work. Together we could change an entire industry!

And, in fact, Saturn's launch proved one of the most impressive brand debuts in the history of the auto industry. Within four years, Saturn

- was number two in overall retail sales in America,
- was number one in dealer satisfaction according to the main arbiter, J.D. Power and Associates,
- had the highest resale value (percent of sticker price) of any car in any class,
- had the highest customer-retention rate in the automobile industry, and
- had the highest sales per retailer of any brand in the industry.

However, the statistic that meant the most to me—and that has the most to do with my contention that leading with love is the best way to run any organization—was that Saturn was number one in overall customer satisfaction. Not just for small cars, but for the entire automotive industry. This was remarkable for several reasons. First, Saturn's sales and delivery process out-scored high-priced luxury brands such as Infiniti, Lexus, and Mercedes-Benz. In fact, Saturn surpassed the previous highest score J.D. Power had ever recorded.

Second, more than 90 percent of Saturn owners were "very satisfied" with the way their cars were sold and delivered, even though the vast majority of American car buyers found the industry's overall process highly distasteful. Saturn buyers began to demand the same treatment from other brands, and soon "Saturnizing" became a verb that other companies attempted with varying degrees of success.

What Saturn was accomplishing was really my mother's advice extended across an entire organization. *Make their day better*—not because you have a mushy need to be liked or to be softhearted, but because it works! I had a unique perspective of Saturn because I left Saturn "corporate" after the launch of the first car to run (and partially own) four Saturn retail outlets as part of the Serra Automotive Group. I wanted to see Saturn from the front line.

I had seen the effect of Skip LeFauve's strong belief in kindness instilled in the corporate leaders, field organization, and plant workers who were enthused about their jobs. After I moved to the dealership level where the rubber hit the road, literally, I witnessed the same kindness and enthusiasm. The dealership owners, the Serras, believed in the mission and were kind and respectful to their sales and service team members who in turn treated the final customer well.

I later returned to Saturn's corporate headquarters as a regional manager to complete my journey of seeing kindness living and breathing at every level of Saturn, from the CEO to the mechanic servicing the cars. Kindness was very real—and very successful!

Kindness Works

So, as I stood in the rain on that hot summer day in Tennessee and watched complete strangers hug one another because they loved our brand, I had a surreal feeling. We had come so far in such a short time.

I realized I was experiencing the *essence* of customer enthusiasm and the *product* of kindness.

The Saturn enthusiasts wanted to talk with plant technicians who had built their cars. They asked to sign their names on the white brick walls of the Saturn plant. They had been treated with trust and respect, and they were rewarding us with their car-purchase dollars. This translated into loyalty too — everyone I talked with wanted to buy another Saturn. We were hitting the bull's-eye.

I learned a vital principle from this remarkable experience: *the enthusiasm of the guest experience can never rise any higher than the enthusiasm of your own employees.*

Saturn leaders were passionate, the Saturn employees calling on dealers were passionate, and the dealers were passionate, transferring that enthusiasm to their own salespeople and service technicians. Everyone was out to achieve a clearly defined mission; and it started with the kindness of our leader, Skip LeFauve.

Kindness is a critical component of organizational success, but being an encourager and being enthusiastic does not make you a Pollyanna. I'm not asking your organization to sing "Kumbaya" around a campfire. Kindness is about intentionally creating and maintaining the right environment in your organization so that frontline employees can deliver an enthusiastic guest experience. Management is kind to employees, employees are kind to customers, and customers are loyal and enthusiastic. Everybody wins. I know this isn't rocket science, but it is hard to execute and takes unending leadership focus and energy, which is why more organizations don't pull it off.

In my non-Saturn experience at GM, I witnessed some leaders who distrusted dealers and failed to treat them with the kindness and respect they were due. In turn, I witnessed some dealers who treated salespeople like they were incompetent and customers as objects ripe for exploitation. Saturn dealers were hardened businesspeople who had decades of experience in a flawed business model—and then they were given the chance to change it with kindness; and they did.

At Herschend Family Entertainment we specifically focus on creating an enthused workforce that treats the end consumer with kindness. We know this works, because we are consistently rated among the friendliest parks in the industry. All employees (including leaders) are given a kindness rating as part of their annual review, a rating that measures enthusiasm, passion, and encouragement. We employ both a kindness metric and a corporate-wide expectation that leaders demonstrate passion and enthusiasm.

We do all this because it sets the tone for the entire organization. Kindness isn't an add-on—it's a critical component of any well-run organization. Kindness is the root of encouragement, encouragement leads to enthusiasm, and everyone benefits.

4.3

The Note

I was having a particularly bad day in 2009. The recession was in full gear, and attendance numbers at our parks were headed in the wrong direction. We had also been working for more than a year on two acquisitions that had just fallen through. As a result, our meetings were spent cutting expenses, trimming capital expenditures, and making other agonizing decisions.

It was a bad day in a bad month in a bad year, and I was feeling low, struggling to determine what we could do to get things headed back in the right direction.

I opened the mail that day without enthusiasm, only to find a note from Jack. It read:

> Joel, as you said, '09 has been a tough year and I agree. In some respects it has been a great year in that you and your team have proved that you can manage thru the toughest times you are likely to experience the rest of your career. Thank you for the awesome jacket and the kind words.
>
> Jack

His note was exactly what I needed. It inspired me and fed my need for a boost. The power of his kind encouragement helped me redouble my efforts to solve our problems and move our company in a positive direction. Jack didn't berate me for what was going wrong—he encouraged me about what was going right.

HERSCHEND FAMILY ENTERTAINMENT

Jack Herschend

Joel,

As you said, 09 has been a tough year and I agree. In some respects it has been a great year in that you and your team have proved that you can manage thru the toughest times you are likely to experience the rest of your career.

Thank you for the awesome jacket and the kind words

...creating memories worth repeating...
Herschend Family Entertainment Corporation

Jack

Of course, that meant longer hours at the office, more missed family dinners, more travel, and more distance between my family and work. Then, about six months later, Marki also got a handwritten note from Jack. As we sat down for a late dinner that night, she read it to me.

Dear Marki, Lauren, Erinn, Jesse and Anna,

Over the last 2 days I had the privilege of watching your dad provide the most awesome leadership to the President's team. It was the kind of leadership that leads to actions pleasing to Jesus. I'm soooo grateful you all choose to share him with us.

Appreciatively,
Jack

Marki said to me, "He's amazing! You've worked in business almost thirty years, and I've *never* gotten a letter from one of your bosses."

A few months later, I received a very attractive offer to run another company that would have paid more than double what I was making at Herschend Family Entertainment. As we were talking through the possibility, Marki said, "Could you really tell Jack, Peter, or the board you're leaving? You've never been in such a supportive environment, and you love what you do—why would you leave?"

That was sage advice from a wise wife. The last time I had made a decision to change jobs mostly for the money, it had been a disaster. I decided to stay, and I'm glad I did. Money can never buy contentment at home; nor can it buy passion at your job. Working with an enthusiastic team and being supported by kind, loving coworkers is priceless.

When, soon after deciding to stay at HFE, I received yet another note from Jack, I felt disappointed in myself. *Jack has written me three notes*, I thought, *and I haven't written one of my own! Why don't I encourage people more?*

HERSCHEND FAMILY ENTERTAINMENT

Jack Herschend

Dear Markie, Lauren, Erinn, Jesse and anna,

over the last 2 days I had the privilege of watching your Dad provide the most awesome leadership to the President's team. It was the kind of leadership that leads to actions pleasing to Jesus.

I'm soooo grateful you all choose to share him with us.

appreciatively,

Jack.

Write 'Em Up!

One reason I was failing to encourage others is that we type A personalities tend to be so concerned with taking the next hill and leading the next charge that we forget to pause and thank the people who are helping us get there.

Second, active encouragement is rarely modeled. I had seen only infrequent glimpses of it until I began to work at HFE. Even before I entered the working world, I didn't often see it at home. My father loved me, and I knew he was proud of me, yet he didn't express those feelings in words. He showed me his love by working hard for the family and attending my games and events, which I appreciated deeply. But I had to *learn* the power of active encouragement later in life.

I called Jack and asked, "How do you do it? We're all busy with conflicts and demands on our time, so how do you always seem to write the perfect note at the perfect time?"

Jack's answer shed light on how to practice kindness. "I spend the first twenty minutes of my morning reflecting on the day before," he told me. "I think about what behavior I saw that should be encouraged, and then I write a note to reinforce it and to say thanks."

Take Time to Encourage

What a powerful thought: spend part of every day actively encouraging behavior you want to reinforce! When I focus my first efforts of the day on writing encouraging notes, it puts me in a positive frame of mind to start the day—so I'm a beneficiary along with my employees. In fact, I've come to believe that the definition of CEO needs to be expanded. It also stands for "chief encouragement officer," for this is a vital responsibility for any executive.

As I walk the halls of our park offices, I see notes everywhere from Jack and Peter. They may be framed on walls, taped to the edge of computer monitors, or displayed in scrapbooks, but all are kept because all are special.

Encouragement can take other forms as well: it may be words of praise, quality time, a small gift, or perhaps an act of service. The point is to be a chief encouragement officer for your organization. Kindness in the context of leading with love begins with you—encouragement and enthusiasm start at the top whether you run the local PTA or a Fortune 500 company.

Does your organization need you to transform the term "write 'em up" into something to look forward to? How do people feel after interactions with you—inspired or deflated? Will active encouragement inspire your team and excite your customers? Being kind starts with you and is a key attribute of leading with love. How will you spend the first twenty minutes of *your* day tomorrow?

Kind
Chapter Summary

☑ Kind: show encouragement and enthusiasm.

☑ The enthusiasm of the guest experience can never rise higher than the enthusiasm of your employees.
  - Kindness, encouragement, and enthusiasm start at the top.
  - When a leader is kind, it will influence front-line employees who interact directly with the customers.

☑ Make their day better.
  - Every time you contact someone, you can make their day better or worse — so make it better.
  - Making a day "better" sometimes requires very little action or effort.

☑ Write 'em up.
  - Break through the email clutter and use hand-written notes of thanks.
  - Begin each day reflecting on the previous day, thinking about what you want to reinforce. Consider writing supporting notes to spouses as well.
  - CEO = chief encouragement officer. All of us can be a "CEO" under those terms.

5

TRUSTING
PLACE CONFIDENCE IN SOMEONE

We're never so vulnerable than when we
trust someone—but paradoxically, if we
cannot trust, neither can we find love or joy.
Walter Anderson

Jack and Peter Herschend made a decision long ago to trust people until proven wrong. Choosing to trust people is a decision we make, a decision that stems from how we view life. Since trust is at the heart of healthy relationships, businesses and individuals both flourish in an atmosphere of trust.

Some people are not trustworthy, true. But to become a great leader, one needs to assume the best about each person. Trusting the people we work with is crucial to building a climate of positive morale and successful performance. Trust can take many forms, and some will surprise you, but the bottom line is that successful leaders understand and activate trust on a daily basis.

- Do you wish you knew how to create a more trusting environment in your organization?
- Have you ever considered poor listening as a sign of distrust?
- How can you remain passionate and engaged while not showing signs of distrust by micromanaging?
- What if trust could make a day-to-day difference at your work?

5.1

Miss Pray

Miss Pray was my seventh-grade teacher at Woodrow Junior High School in Battle Creek, Michigan. She was in her seventies back then but sharp as a tack. Her thick white hair was always perfectly groomed, and her skin was taut across her strong cheekbones. She was intense, a disciplinarian who didn't choose to smile much. And I loved her—she was a wonderful instructor.

One day Mom and I attended my parent-teacher conference together with Miss Pray. It wasn't normal for the student to attend, but Miss Pray had requested my presence. I assumed it was going to be a great meeting. Perhaps she would bestow some kind of honor on me; after all, I had straight As and perfect attendance.

Miss Pray began the meeting by speaking directly to my mother and explaining that I was an excellent student. She said I grasped concepts quickly and was able to apply them in various situations. She appreciated my focus, attendance, and behavior while she was teaching. Things were going just as I'd expected.

Suddenly my eyes widened when she said, "Mrs. Manby, I wanted Joel to be here so we could discuss an issue together. I would like to speak to him directly, but I wanted you here so you could hear my words and help Joel become a better person."

Miss Pray—
a listening mentor.

Forty years later, thinking about that conversation still opens a pit in my stomach. It came as a complete shock, and I had no clue what she was about to say. Miss Pray looked directly at me. "Joel, you are a gifted leader. I have seen many people come through these halls, and you are at the very top in your ability to gain people's trust, take control of a situation, rally those around you, and get things done."

I still wondered where all this was headed. So far it sounded pretty good, but I knew more was coming. Miss Pray continued, "However, you are a very poor listener. I have watched you take over a class group project when you were not even assigned to be the leader. Then, what's worse, you didn't listen to others in the group when they tried to speak. You interrupted them and often cut them off."

She wasn't finished. "I have also watched you on the kickball field during intramurals. You weren't the captain, but you took over and wouldn't listen to people — you just directed them where to go. Your friend Jeff was very upset because you wouldn't listen to his thoughts about who should play where."

As the truth of her words began to sink in, she made her closing statement. "Joel, when you don't listen to others, it sends them a very negative and unflattering message. You are telling them they are not important. You are telling them you are better than they are. You have the natural ability to be a great leader, but you are going to have to fix your listening skills or you will be limited in how far you can go."

I sat there in silence, a bit stunned. I felt horrible, and deep down I knew her assessment was accurate. Mom thanked Miss Pray for her care and concern, and we left. I never forgot that day.

Miss Pray cared enough to call me out, and that made me a better leader going forward. I was failing to trust my classmates and friends, and that failure would have crippled my ability to lead.

Trust Me

Miss Pray was right. When we interrupt or respond without taking account of what others have said, we send several messages — none of them good:

- My idea is greater than your idea, so I don't have to listen.
- Interrupting you is okay because your response isn't that important.
- I'm not listening to you because I'm already preparing my response.

The truth is this: *interrupting is a sign of distrust.*

That's a strong statement, but it's undeniable. Hard-driving leaders who often interrupt will always justify their behavior. "I already know where that person's headed, and I want to save time." Or, "I'm just efficient and don't have time to waste." If interruption is seen as simply being rude, many leaders don't think it needs to be changed — a little rudeness in an organization isn't the end of the world. However, when leaders understand that interrupting others shows a lack of trust, the notion of interruptions gains significance.

Would your employees or coworkers rate you as a good listener or a poor listener? Would they say you listen without interrupting? Would they say you hear them? If you struggle with listening well, as I did early in my life and career, these simple steps can help:

1. Don't say, "I understand how you feel, but ..." Most people won't feel that you understand, especially if you discount their thinking and immediately move in a different direction.

2. Instead, summarize what you have heard. If you really
   trust them, they will agree with your summary and feel
   as if their idea has been given a fair hearing.
3. If you go a different direction, articulate why. Always
   try to explain your logic when differing with some of
   your team. They may not agree, and that's okay, but
   you'll all know what everyone is thinking.

Listening well is critical because it demonstrates trust and
builds a team's sense of camaraderie and cohesion. Poor listening
is more than forgivable rudeness: it's a breach of trust and not a
quality of leading with love.

5.2

Gene

I have interviewed hundreds of people in my thirty plus years in business, and I have seen almost every situation imaginable. However, over lunch with Gene, who was being interviewed for a senior leadership position at Herschend Family Entertainment, I saw something new.

Our lunch was going very well. He was working for a larger competitor, and he clearly knew his field of expertise. Not only that, but he seemed to like our direction, growth strategy, and culture. As we talked, however, I couldn't understand why Gene was interested in joining the HFE team. He already had a great job that paid very well, and joining us would probably require a pay cut and moving his family.

"Gene, you don't need to sell me any more on your capabilities," I said. "It's clear you have the skills and the drive that we need. But why do you want to leave the company you're with?"

He looked at me, and tears welled up in his eyes. With his voice quivering, he said, "They cut one-third of my team in a mass layoff." And after a long pause, he continued slowly, "And they didn't even ask my opinion. They didn't trust me enough to ask me." Then he was silent. He could no longer speak without crying.

Gene's leaders lost his trust because they made a major decision without his input. He was willing to leave his company because of a lack of trust. One of the best ways a leader can demonstrate trust and respect is to listen to and involve team members in the decisions that affect them.

Saturn's Ring of Trust

I have seen the good, the bad, and the ugly when it comes to involving others in decisions that affect them. Long before I met Gene, I saw this principle play out with frontline workers in the auto industry, both for good and ill. Involving those in decisions that affect them is not just for senior leaders; it applies to all levels of the organization. At Saturn, for instance—whose stated core values included trust and respect for others—there was a tremendous relationship between the UAW union workers in the plant and the nonunion management.

The UAW had representatives on the Saturn board of directors, and the union's involvement in Saturn was critical from board-level strategy to decisions about the production facility in Spring Hill. The UAW members worked hard and were diligent and enthusiastic. They wanted Saturn to succeed as much as the leadership did. The trust at work extended past working hours, and we would even hang out together in social situations.

People want to be involved in decisions that affect them because they understand that participation is a sign of trust from leadership.

This doesn't always mean that decisions are made by an organization-wide committee, but those affected by any decision at least should enjoy some input and be able to understand why a decision was made.

I clearly remember one Saturn board meeting where I presented our launch strategy to about seventeen people, a combination of Saturn and UAW senior leaders. As I gave my presentation,

I realized I didn't know several of the people. I still remember thinking, *I don't know who's who here, management or union.*

I was impressed. No one wore a tie, everyone dressed the same, and all of the board members were equally energetic and asked great questions. Clearly, decisions were being made as a team in an environment of trust. That translated to happier, more enthusiastic workers at all levels and a thriving company, proving that trust pays dividends.

Distrust at a GM Truck Plant

Juxtapose my Saturn experience with what I saw in my first job out of college. I was a plant foreman at a GM truck plant in Pontiac, Michigan. It was a horrible—but valuable—experience.

There the line between the union and senior leaders was stark. The UAW's relationship with management was adversarial. This animosity had built up over the decades and even passed on from generation to generation. All management had to wear ties and white shirts on the plant floor, while the UAW members wore jeans or overalls.

The UAW called us "suits" and had little desire to interact with management in any way, shape, or form. I felt as if they wouldn't even give me a chance to get to know them because my tie marked me as an enemy. I felt as if they hated me before I ever said my first word.

A few members of my production team would get drunk at lunch and use their breaks to sleep in big cardboard boxes in the back of the plant, often not coming back from breaks on time— if at all! I continually witnessed the lack of respect with which the workers approached their jobs.

One Saturday after being short a few workers all week, I was looking forward to playing golf to get away from it all. Imagine my surprise when a player assigned to our foursome was one of the UAW workers from my line—the same man who was out of work on long-term disability with a note from his doctor stating that he couldn't work because of his severe headaches. His headache seemed to be okay as he joked around with his buddies on the first tee.

When he saw me walk up, he scoffed and said, "Talk to my union rep on Monday."

I decided to wait for the next tee time!

I hated my experience on that plant floor and couldn't wait to get out. Mind you, this was thirty years ago in one isolated plant. Since then, however, I've wondered about the causes of that toxic work environment. Were those workers always so distrustful and apathetic, or was their attitude shaped over time by decisions that the management made?

One thing is clear about my time at that plant: decisions were being made *for* the workers and not *with* them. What was the difference between that and Saturn? After all, it was the same UAW with different results—the same kind of men with a different work ethic.

Trust.

At Saturn, decisions were made *with* the union. At the truck plant, decisions were made *for* the union. At Saturn, all involved parties were consulted and listened to. At the truck plant, the floor workers were expected simply to obey.

The result of such trust was that at Saturn there was a genuine harmony across the labor-management divide, a harmony that led to the manufacture of a beloved product that became a hit with American car buyers. The story of why Saturn didn't last within GM's hierarchy is a lengthy tale for a different time, an example of leadership failure given Saturn's tremendous early success.

However, the positive lessons from Saturn should be remembered and used to transform and improve our organizations today. If we want our organizations to display trust and respect, we need to make sure everyone is involved in the decisions that affect them. The best decisions are always made *with*, not *for*, and showing that kind of trust is a true attribute of leading with love.

5.3

A Tool
for Trust

Deciding that people should be involved in decisions that affect them is the "easy" part — what is harder is making sure the *right* people are involved in decisions and then clearly communicating the decisions to everyone affected by them.

The best method I've seen to clarify this sometimes mundane process can be remembered by a catchy acronym: RACI.

Here's how RACI works. Start by identifying who is *responsible* for the decision. After receiving all available input and doing the required analysis, they're the ones who actually have to decide. What comes next in the process are those who have to *approve* whatever decision is made. They need to approve that the decision is wise and appropriate. However, before the decision becomes final, it's necessary to *consult* the people who will be directly affected by the decision. They may be in other departments or branches of the organization, but trust dictates that they are consulted. Finally, the organization must find the best way to *inform* the rest of the team — people who may not be directly affected but should be kept "in the picture."

This straightforward model is easy to understand and use, yet many leaders don't take the time to specifically define the four elements of RACI up front—and even if they do, they don't always ensure it is executed. It is critical to define the key decisions of a company so the correct teams or people are involved at every level of the RACI hierarchy—this is *always* time well spent, because it builds trust and therefore effectiveness at every level of an organization.

When I first arrived at Herschend Family Entertainment, the RACI process was extremely helpful. When we were small, we were totally decentralized with almost no common processes between parks. Our pay structures were different, benefits varied, and we purchased from the same suppliers with no consolidation for cost savings. Therefore, whenever we chose to centralize—to increase quality or decrease costs—we had to employ the RACI method to assure the parks still felt involved in the decisions they formerly made themselves. They needed to understand why we were making the decisions and feel like they were trusted partners in the process.

The chart below is an actual graphic used at HFE for an employee-benefits decision and is a simple example of how to use RACI.

Function	R Responsible	A Approve	C Consult	I Inform
	Owns the recommen-dation "The doer"	Owns the decision "Buck stops here"	Should be consulted "Keep in the loop"	Should be informed "Keep in the picture"
HFE benefits package content	HFE corporate benefits team	HFE benefits advisory committee	HFE corporate HR Property HR directors	All HFE employees

In this example, we had a specific dollar amount we were willing to spend on benefits. Instead of the HFE corporate benefits team making the decision on its own regarding what to cut or add to our benefit package, it spent a great deal of time consulting with the property HR directors to assure we reached the highest value package for our employees. Even though we ended up spending less on benefits due to budget constraints, we cut the least important areas and were able to add better wellness initiatives and the increased flexibility for time off that our employees wanted. As a result, we got a better response from our employees, because we trusted our specific property leaders to make the best decision for local employees.

By using this RACI approach, we have been able to effectively move from being completely decentralized to centralizing decisions when it makes sense. In our experience, if the different HFE teams or properties understand they are a part of the decision-making process and know the role they are playing, it diffuses a lot of the confusion, poor decisions, and hurt feelings along the way.

Efficiency vs. Effectiveness

Although autocratic decision making is faster — and therefore far more efficient — it is almost always less effective, because others in the organization may not support the decision. As a result, team members can help "make it fail" in their own unique ways, and they certainly won't be as energetic about the unilateral decision. A leader may decide something, but the whole organization needs to execute it.

Using RACI to involve others in decisions that affect them will sometimes prolong decision making. However, when team members know they are trusted enough to be part of the decision-making process in advance, their support of the decision will be stronger and the implementation of that decision will be faster and more effective.

We think we want efficient organizations, but what we really want is *effective* organizations.

Decisions made autocratically

Decision time	Implementation time

Decisions made by those affected

Decision time	Implementation time

What's amazing about trust is that it can be both effective and efficient. The total time required both to *decide* and *implement* is actually shorter when we involve the necessary team members. This is an unexpected benefit of trusting leadership. When people aren't involved in the decisions that affect them, implementation can slow to a crawl and use more time and resources than a fully informed decision-making process.

We cannot lead with love without trust. Trust your team, and your team will trust you. Using a RACI chart can help you do that—and help your organization thrive in the process.

5.4

The Chairman

Nelson Schwab is the current chairman of Herschend Family Entertainment, taking over when I became CEO in 2003 (HFE requires the nonexecutive board chair and CEO to be two different people). He is a tremendous leader with a solid track record and a laser-sharp business mind, and a large portion of HFE's success can be attributed to Nelson's steady presence on the board for more than a quarter century.

Nelson is also a leader who understands the value of trust. As smart and capable as he is, he lets me make the decisions I'm responsible for. When we talk, he gives me input, but he always makes it clear that it's my decision. On the other hand, I have so much respect for Nelson's experience and wisdom that I'd be ill-advised to ignore his input — trust works both ways!

About a year ago, we were considering splitting HFE into two entities. One entity would be growth oriented and take on more debt to acquire properties, while the other entity would be more conservative and keep debt levels low. This would allow shareholders to invest in the entity they were the most comfortable with. It was a sophisticated transaction with multiple and complicated tax issues.

I was on the phone with Nelson discussing it, and he said, "I applaud Andrew [our CFO] and you for bringing this idea forward. It's a complex deal, so get the best opinion available on the tax issues. Also, speak with the family representatives on the board to make sure they're comfortable with this. And look at the worst-case scenario and make sure you can live with it. Once you come to your recommendation, let's talk before the board meeting."

Your recommendation.

What a freeing thought! However, I could tell by his energy and the questions he asked that he thought the idea was too big of a step for the company at this stage. Still, he didn't shut me down; he let me make the recommendation.

His advice was on target. The two best law firms in Atlanta were split on the ability to get past the negative tax issues — a large red flag.

When I spoke with the various family members at the shareholders meeting, I could tell they were all trying to be supportive, but a sense of nervousness about the worst-case scenario filled the room. Another red flag.

So, after all our due diligence, Andrew and I made the recommendation to pass on splitting HFE. Along the way, we involved the right people before we made our recommendation. If Nelson had shut me down immediately, as he probably felt like doing, I always would have wondered if we had missed out on a big opportunity to grow faster than our current structure allows. RACI — and trust — are the keys to effective decision making.

In the years I have worked with Nelson, Jack, and Peter, I have learned at least two key points from them about trust-filled decision making:

1. *Let others make the decisions for which they are responsible.*
   A leader must choose carefully when he or she is going to step in and get involved in decision-making details. If done too often, it shows a lack of trust — and if the team is talented, they will sense the leader's distrust and may even leave the company.

2. *Avoid overruling decisions that have been made.* Clearly, if the downside of the potential error is very expensive or puts the organization at risk, a leader must step in. However, day in and day out, many issues and problems can be solved using less intrusive approaches. Trustful leaders must let people do their jobs, find their own solutions, and even make occasional mistakes in order to learn.

Unfortunately, not all leaders have integrity, and some have violated, or will violate, our trust. However, being a great leader in any organization starts with one's assumptions about human beings: Do you trust them or not? If you inherently trust others and believe they want to do their best and get better, you can become a great leader — as long as you hire talented self-starters.

If you inherently distrust people and believe they are trying to do as little as possible or just do enough to get by, leading will be difficult. Such distrustful leadership will result in low performance and high turnover.

Whenever I interview a potential leader, I always ask, "Do you trust that employees will always do their best?"

If they say something like "I feel like people will always take advantage of you if you don't watch them" or "I like to closely monitor my team," I end the interview as quickly as possible. These aren't the kind of leaders I want working for me or representing HFE.

Trust is the key to any healthy relationship — whether at home or in a business or organization. If we trust others or we want to trust others more, we will listen well, involve our team in decisions that affect them, and trust them to make the decisions they are paid to make.

Leading with love isn't possible if you don't trust people. And when you do trust people, leading will be more effective than ever.

Trusting
Chapter Summary

☑ Trusting: place confidence in someone.

☑ Listening carefully is a sign of trust. Interrupting people is a sign of distrust.

☑ RACI is a trust tool to involve others in the decisions that affect them.
  • Use it to clarify who needs to be involved in a decision.
  • Although involving those affected by a decision may take more time than an autocratic decision, the total time through implementation will usually be shorter.

☑ Don't just *define* the decision making process — *follow* it.
  • Let others make the decisions they are responsible for.
  • Avoid overriding a decision that has already been made unless it is absolutely necessary.

6

UNSELFISH
THINK OF YOURSELF LESS

Being in power is like being a lady. If you have to remind people that you are, you aren't.

Margaret Thatcher

Being unselfish doesn't mean thinking *less* of yourself — it means thinking *of* yourself less. When you're selfish, you insist on your own way with every decision because you're thinking of yourself. The unfortunate reality is that we are all selfish to a degree — that's human nature. Is there anyone more selfish than a baby?

What matters, then, is to mature. No leader should continue to make "baby" decisions, but instead should strive for a mature — and unselfish — leadership style. Isn't that the kind of leader you love to follow?

The difficult journey of life is to move from a *selfish* heart to a *serving* heart. We become mature adults when we understand — finally — that our organizations, just like our lives, are more about what we give than what we get.

Selfish leaders need to remind people that they are in power, and they like to hold on to power instead of giving it away. They are selfish with their own treasure, time, and talent, and they take that selfish heart to work with them each day. Those organizations, and the people working there, are invariably worse off. An unselfish leader, however, can literally transform an organization. I've seen it happen.

- Do you give generously of your personal time, treasure, and talent?
- Have you ever wanted to make things less about yourself and more about your team?
- Have you considered the link between personal unselfishness and organizational unselfishness?
- Does helping everyone seem so overwhelming that you help no one?

6.1

Glenn

It was a hot summer night in Battle Creek, and the city's twelve and under Little League baseball championship was on the line at Greenfield Park. The stands were packed with cheering parents. Two outs, bases loaded, and my team was down by two runs in the bottom of the final inning.

Guess who was stepping up to the plate.

I had struck out my two previous times at bat, so I wasn't exactly brimming with confidence, but the opposing pitcher had just walked a batter to load the bases. I told myself, "Just make contact and don't swing too hard—he's going to throw a strike."

The first pitch came right down the middle, and I swung. *Crack!*

I made solid contact and drove the ball over the fence and into the windshield of an unsuspecting car! My grand-slam home run won the game 7–5 and gave us the championship. I felt like I was floating on air as I circled the bases.

Our team decided to celebrate by going to A&W for root beer and ice cream. But my dad surprised me when he said, "Sorry, we can't go—I have to get home for a mowing job."

That was all he said. I was extremely upset and disappointed, but I didn't say anything for fear of getting in trouble. We climbed

Manby Farm Machinery in Battle Creek, Michigan (c. 1965).

into our car and drove one direction while the rest of the team headed out to celebrate.

It was a quiet ride home.

As I went to bed that night, my mom came into my room to say goodnight. She noticed my tear-stained face and said: "You know, your father is very proud of you; you did a great job in that game."

I looked up at her and asked, "Why doesn't Dad love me? Why wouldn't he take me to get root beer with everyone else?"

I'll never forget what Mom said. "Joel, your father has a payroll to meet tomorrow at the dealership, and he doesn't have any money to spare. He needs to pay his staff. Things are very tight right now. Your dad feels badly about this. It's hard for him to talk about, but the dealership isn't doing well, and he's doing the very best he can."

That was the first time I realized just how bad things were for our family financially. Dad owned and ran an Oliver agricultural dealership in Battle Creek called Manby Farm Machinery. He was hardworking, but Oliver just wasn't able to compete with John Deere—and a general consolidation of small farm equipment dealerships in the Midwest was also working against him.

I found out later that during that period, Dad could only

bring home about $50 a week because the dealership was performing so poorly. Even in the mid–1960s, $2,600 a year didn't go nearly far enough. But my father refused to ask for government assistance, so we struggled on until the dealership closed.

Personal Unselfishness

As a young boy, I had a clear understanding that my dad was unselfish, that he gave all he had to make things work financially. He didn't have time for hobbies and never had many friends. He simply worked.

Yet I never knew the extent of his selflessness until after he died of cancer at the age of eighty. After the funeral, we had a gathering at my childhood home that included family and close friends. Story after story about my dad came flowing out, changing forever the way I would understand his generosity. Many of the stories I had never heard before, and the anecdotes spoke to his caring heart, his gentle spirit, and his work ethic.

Dad's brother, Uncle Bob, told us that in World War II both he and my father enlisted, but Dad got sent home after basic training to work the family farm because the military deemed that generating crops was my father's highest and best use.

His sister, Jean, said, "Your dad felt guilty about being sent home to work on the farm. He knew his brother was fighting in the war, and your dad felt like he needed to make up for it."

After pausing for a few minutes, she continued, saying, "John worked harder than three normal men. He worked a seventy-five-acre farm by himself—planting, harvesting, and taking care of the cows. Our father was too ill, and I wasn't much help. He nearly worked himself to death making that farm go. I've never seen anyone work that hard and that long."

As my aunt reminisced, other pictures raced through my memory from my childhood.

After working a long day, my father would always plow the snow from our neighbor's driveway for free because her husband had been killed in an industrial accident. Dad didn't have much cash to give others, but he was unselfish with what he did have—his hours and his Oliver 55 tractor.

Then the doorbell rang, and I opened it to find Glenn, my dad's only employee toward the end of the Oliver dealership's existence. Glenn had come to tell us all a story. "I worked hard as a mechanic for your father," he said. "Fifteen years in total. But try as we might, we couldn't keep the doors to that dealership open."

He continued: "After the dealership closed for good, your father did something incredible. I know how broke he was. It was as tough for him as it was for me, yet he continued to pay me for more than three months until I found another job. He helped me hold it together during a very difficult time. He was a great man. He was generous, and he cared. I've worked at many other places since then, but I want all of you kids to know that I never worked for a finer man."

I thought deeply about what Glenn had said. Dad's dream was to build a viable business, and he pursued it by working six or seven days a week for years, from sunup to sundown, struggling to make it work even after its demise became inevitable. Once it closed, he had no source of income, and it took him six months to land his next job as a factory worker. Yet Dad felt such an obliga-

That's me on the lawn mower with Glenn (left) and my father in front of Manby Farm Machinery.

tion to the one man he employed that he continued to pay Glenn from his paltry savings until he found another job.

Give 'Til It Helps

My father was the definition of unselfish. Dad cared about other people enough to give his own resources to help them. He was generous and compassionate, and to this day I hope to follow his example in my own life.

You may ask what personal unselfishness has to do with leading. It's simple. If we are unable to be selfless in our personal life, we are unlikely to be unselfish as a leader, and unselfishness is a key component of leading with love.

Giving our time and talents is a concept shared by many philosophies and religions, including Christianity, Islam, and Judaism. However, I believe that giving is critical as a leader, regardless of your personal beliefs. This is because leading effectively requires leaders to

- think of others
- remind themselves that any leadership position is a gift
- reject the rat race of chasing possessions
- choose to be unselfish

There are many ways that we as people and leaders can be unselfish. We can't all give the same things in the same ways. However, there are some general concepts about giving that almost anyone can implement. Much like the RACI tool, the following principles will help you evaluate the best ways to "share it forward" in your personal life, which will position and train you to be a more unselfish leader in your organization.

Treasure: Give a percent of your income off the top.
The first key to developing an unselfish attitude is to give before you spend. Marki and I give a certain percentage of our annual

income and follow a progressive giving schedule—the more we make, the higher percentage we give. Determining the percent up front helped us loosen our grip on money in two ways. First, we always give a certain percent of our income before we spend other money, and we've shared that intent with our accountant, who helps keep us accountable. Second, we've established an upper limit to our net worth—once we cross that line, we'll give away all of what we make. These principles assure that "lifestyle creep" doesn't reduce our giving over time.

Talent: Give your skills to make the world better.

I see many at HFE following this principle. Jack and Peter lead by example and are generous and passionate about personal giving. For instance, Peter has been fighting against multiple sclerosis for more than twenty-five years. To date he has raised over 1.5 million dollars with his passion for riding bicycles and his ability to network. His clear personal investment in this cause inspires others around him to give of their own talents. It is possible to give money to a cause without really caring about it, but the moment we dedicate our skills and talents to a cause, we prove we are invested and inspire those around us to do the same.

Time: Give whatever you have been blessed with.

Beyond money and talent, consider the simple gift of your time. What does your weekly and yearly calendar look like? Is there a place for helping others built into your schedule? If there isn't, it's not going to "just happen." My father is a good example. He gave much of his time, yet to the outside world it appeared he had little to give. He didn't have money or successful business experience to share, but he did have time, a big heart, a strong body, and an Oliver 55 tractor. He gave generously of those assets to those around him, and those who knew him—who watched him plow the snow from their driveways, for example—will never forget him.

What If?

The crazy thing about giving is this: when we give, we never know what might happen. Often giving provides the *giver* with unexpected blessings—as well as making the world a better place.

Consider the story of Adam Braun, a twenty-two-year-old college graduate who was backpacking in a small village in India when a group of children ran up to him, hoping for a gift of some kind. All Adam could find in his backpack was a pencil. That seemed like such a paltry, pitiful gift, but he was backpacking ... what else could he give? Feeling sheepish, Adam still gave the pencil to one of the children.

The child's eyes lit up like the sun!

When Adam saw the joyous reaction to such a seemingly insignificant gift, he thought, *If this little girl responds so strongly to a pencil, I wonder how she would respond to a new school?*

What started as a thought soon became a dream—and before long that dream became Adam's passion. That young man founded Pencils of Promise, a nonprofit that builds schools in developing countries (www.pencilsofpromise.org). Adam is one of the new wave of social entrepreneurs doing amazing things through giving—and he'll tell you that he has never been happier or more fulfilled.

My dad, the Herschends, Adam Braun, and millions around the world give what they can personally. They intentionally pass on their time, their talent, and their treasure to others, knowing that in giving they will always gain more than they lose.

What about you? How unselfish are you?

Be unselfish with your time, talents, and treasure *now*, not *someday*. There's no doubt that giving will make you a more complete and caring person—and that will make you a better leader. Too often we check our giving at the office door, thinking that work is no place to be generous.

The exact opposite is true, and that's the subject of the next chapter.

6.2

Monica

As I toured Wild Adventures, our theme park in Valdosta, Georgia, I was impressed with how nice everything looked. We had purchased the park out of bankruptcy, and it was in poor shape when we got it. Now, four years later, it looked beautiful — in part because Jack Herschend had led a refurbishment team that planted more than five hundred trees and removed — yes, *removed* — more than two thousand tons of concrete to soften the park's feel and add more shade. We sold the concrete to the city of Valdosta, which used the recycled material as a base for new roads — talk about a win-win!

The new landscaping was gorgeous. Flowers shot up colorful fireworks everywhere I looked, and the tree beds were free of weeds. In the middle of the park a brand-new garden with shady benches beckoned weary visitors. So when I saw a landscaper on her knees planting some flowers, I went over to thank her for what I saw. She introduced herself as Monica. I said, "Monica, thank you so much for what you do; these grounds look tremendous!"

She said, "Thank you, sir. But I want to thank *you* for supporting Share It Forward."

"You're welcome," I replied, even though I had no idea exactly what she was thanking me for. Share It Forward, our company foundation to assist employees in need, has helped more than two thousand of our employees and their families since it began, but I wasn't sure where Monica fit in.

As I walked away, the park's general manager, Bob Montgomery, asked, "Do you know Monica's story?"

He proceeded to tell me how Monica's older sister died unexpectedly and left behind a nine-month-old daughter named Layla. Although Monica was only twenty-two and single, she decided to take Layla as her own. At the time, she had only a seasonal job at Wild Adventures, and her parents didn't have the resources to help financially. Herschend Family Entertainment encouraged Monica to apply for help from the Share It Forward Foundation, which agreed to help with the costs of her sister's funeral. In addition, Monica qualified for the single-parent program, so she received a monthly stipend.

Wow! Monica, a single young woman with her entire life in front of her, made a selfless decision to adopt her sister's baby — for life; and Monica's selflessness was aided by HFE's selflessness. Her amazing and inspirational story is one of hundreds written within HFE each year — often with help from HFE's explicit policy of giving more than just paychecks to its employees.

Here I am with Monica, one of the two
thousand individuals or families helped
so far by Share It Forward, at
Wild Adventures in Valdosta, Georgia.

Organizations Need to Be Unselfish Too

Being unselfish isn't just for individuals — it's for organizations too. As leaders we've been blessed with resources, and part of our responsibility is to pass it on or "share it forward." The gift of leadership brings with it the awesome responsibility of giving properly of our time and resources but also of being a steward of giving for the organization.

I've mentioned the Share It Forward Foundation briefly, but there is no single program at HFE that exemplifies personal and organizational unselfishness better than this program. Here is how it works. HFE employees start the momentum with their donations, so without the personal selflessness discussed in the preceding chapter, our most important employee aid program would never get off the ground. The percentage of employees contributing has gone up each year, with Stone Mountain Park in Atlanta, Georgia, leading the way with an 80 percent contribution rate.

We then follow the employees' example with organizational unselfishness; the company matches the employee donations out of profits. Then the Herschend family gives an additional grant, even though they own 100 percent of the company and have already helped by allowing the company to match donations with profit. Now *that's* unselfishness!

As a result of this combined giving, nearly 10 percent of our seasonal employees have received some kind of financial assistance over the last five years. These funds helped them meet an unexpected medical bill, get through a natural disaster, or financially survive some other emergency. For instance, you may have seen the episode of CBS's *Undercover Boss* featuring HFE, which I referenced in the introduction. Richard, the hardworking maintenance worker, received a $10,000 catastrophic aid grant from Share It Forward. His home had been destroyed in a flood, and he had been living in a pop-up trailer with his wife and five children while he saved money to fix his home. The $10,000 allowed Richard to quickly get his life and home back together.

We also provide partial scholarships to employees or their dependents. Albert, whom you also met in the introduction, received one of those scholarships to Valdosta State University. In addition, our child assistance program helps qualifying single parents receive monthly stipends — in the same way Share It Forward did for Monica.

I am so grateful for our foundation and the difference it makes by giving people gifts they need — after all, Share It Forward let Monica keep planting flowers at Wild Adventures *and* adopt and raise Layla. Richard and his family are now back in their home, and Albert is getting a good education so he can be a better leader. When everyone gives, everyone wins.

In case you think it's "easy" for a privately held company to give like this because it isn't beholden to public investors, note that HFE borrowed the idea from two very public companies: The Home Depot and Walmart. These organizations help their employees in need and excel in the dog-eat-dog world of retailing — all the while succeeding under the scrutiny of public ownership.

I unequivocally reject the argument that a foundation like Share It Forward has a negative impact on corporate financial performance. It doesn't. Period.

In fact, the opposite is true. Foundations like Share It Forward create organization-wide loyalty and passion and help maintain an enthusiastic, motivated workforce and satisfied guests. HFE's corporate donations are pre-established at 10 percent of after-tax profits in order to plan cash flow and make an up-front commitment. At HFE we decide how much we will give to assure that we are unselfish with the organization's resources; so the idea of giving a set percent of revenue or income is just as important in an organization as it is in our personal lives. The result of both practices is less selfishness and, in the long term, better organizational results!

In fact, I would argue that the cash we use to help our employees with Share It Forward helps create an enthusiastic, loyal workforce that does more good for our guest experience, dollar for dollar, than our cash investments in our attractions.

Giving simply works — and it's the right thing to do too. Isn't it great when the right thing to do is the smart thing to do as well?

Time and Talent

Giving time and talent to develop internal leaders is another important reflection of being unselfish in an organization. In this case, the recipients of selflessness are the next generation of company leaders. To that end, we have put several leadership programs in place, including one for developing the talent of seasonal workers who have the potential to be supervisors or managers. We assign mentors to these promising seasonal workers to see if they have the leadership skills necessary to succeed at HFE.

For potential senior leaders, the Intense Development Program (IDP) ensures that each developing leader gets a mentor who spends time reviewing a specific career development plan and assures that the employee is "moved along" in the organization so the proper skills are developed. We also run IDP participants through a battery of tests to assess strengths and areas where we need to assist. It takes time and effort to be a mentor for the IDP, but such unselfish leadership ensures motivated employees and a healthy company in the long-term.

Part of this process also includes *informal* mentoring of young leaders and encouraging them along the way. Jane Cooper, our COO, is excellent at grabbing casual meals with up-and-coming leaders, especially women, to make sure they feel supported. This is an important part of being unselfish: taking the time to invest in future leaders. I have seen Jane take very raw talent, women with a high acumen and energy level, and give them support, the perfect dose of increasing responsibility, and plenty of lunch discussions to make sure they don't feel lost or underappreciated in our organization. We have seen a tremendous increase in the number of female leaders in our organization, and Jane has played a significant role in that.

The Rub

Knowing that we should be giving treasure, time, and talent isn't rocket science for an individual or an organization—but it's hard to execute! Here's the rub: even unselfish leaders are crunched for time and treasure.

With organizations downsizing without eliminating work responsibilities, all of us are under more stress and pressure than ever. Forget helping others—we can't even get done what *we* need to do each day. It can be a struggle to find the time and resources to start a Share It Forward–type program or mentor future leaders.

The temptation, then, is to remain distant and grow cold to the needs of our employees. After all, we have numbers to hit and investors to satisfy. Those things are true—but focusing exclusively on that leads us down the road toward cold hearts and a career defined by disinterest. If we become numb to the needs of our employees, their performance and ability to satisfy our customers will diminish over time, compromising the very "numbers" we were obsessed with.

On the other hand, we cannot help everyone. We can't afford it, and even if we could, there isn't enough time. What is a leader to do when a desire to be unselfish and giving seems to conflict with the realities of organizational demands?

From a "treasure" standpoint, HFE solves this issue by linking our giving to profits. The more we make, the more we give. Of course, the opposite is true as well, but this principle means everyone is motivated to succeed so we can give more to employees in need and to our communities.

From a "time" standpoint, I learned an important principle from my friend Andy Stanley. Andy is a pastor who faces this tension every day as he leads a church of over twenty thousand members. He can't help everyone, but he and his team live by this phrase: "Do for one what you wish you could do for everyone."

Isn't that all that can be asked of us? To help those we can help, and not to let the size of the problem prevent us from acting? Andy makes a habit of choosing a few people to help at a deep, personal level. This keeps his heart soft, and it ensures that his whole church has a visible model of selflessness and giving. You don't have to be a math whiz to calculate that if *everyone* in any organization helped one or two people, everyone would have more than enough help!

Could you do the same? What *one* person in your organization could you mentor? What *two* people could you help who are in serious financial hardship?

During *Undercover Boss*, I learned the truth of Andy's principle by remaining close with three of the people we helped on the show. I consistently followed up with them and "went deep" until they got through their individual crisis. I can attest that this principle will help you be unselfish as a leader — and will help the culture of your organization thrive as never before.

6.3

Autocratic
vs. Socratic

I recently told one of our senior executives that I wanted to stay out of a particular meeting because I needed to start making as few decisions as possible.

He looked at me like I had a third eye.

Yet I believe that the fewer decisions we feel we need to make, the stronger a leader we are and the stronger the team we have built. Before I arrived at Saab USA as president and CEO, I had spent fifteen years in the automotive industry—in sales, marketing, production, and the dealership side of the business. That specific experience meant I could lead—or at least I felt I could lead—as an "expert," taking control of the meetings and laying out my plan. I didn't really trust all those who were at Saab when I arrived, because I suspected they were part of the problem, so I wasn't very willing to listen to their opinions. When I led in this "expert" mode, I felt the best way to use my talent was to tell people what to do. I didn't deploy other strong leadership skills, such as identifying problems, listening to others, and building consensus through critical thinking.

Juxtapose that experience with my first few years at HFE. I had no experience in the themed attractions business, so I took an entirely different approach than I had at Saab. I learned to ask better questions, and I was forced to surround myself with people who knew their areas of expertise better than I did. It was an uncomfortable transition for me, and I was clearly out of my comfort zone at first—but it forced me to draw out the best thinking from those around me.

Being Unselfish with Decisions

As a result, I retired my "expert" leadership skills and learned instead to cultivate other skills. These can be defined broadly as "Socratic skills," including the following:

- Asking more questions to draw out and evaluate what other leaders are thinking. Great questions test the wisdom and logic of an idea better than any "expert" opinion can and also develop the person who has to answer the question.
- Facilitating team discussions to help identify problems and suggest solutions. Good leaders can be active participants in this process, but they often speak last and absorb the various opinions and ideas around the room.
- Making the best decision possible after getting the input of the brightest minds most affected by the decision. This process isn't necessarily based on consensus—a good leader must still set the direction if there is disagreement—but nine times out of ten a better decision is made after using Socratic skills.
- Summarizing the discussion and attempting to build and maintain team unity. If a decision is made that goes a different direction than some of the opinions in the room, a good leader explains why so everyone feels heard.

Through this evolution in my leadership style, I learned a very powerful principle: *Socratic leadership attracts and keeps stronger talent than autocratic leadership does.* At HFE I have been able to

attract and keep the strongest team I have ever had in any industry. I try to hire only the best—and then I let them do their jobs.
They know they are critical to HFE's success, they feel trusted,
and they know they are adding value.

Decide to Decide Less

As a leader's seniority increases, that leader should make fewer decisions. As CEO, it's not my job to insert myself in areas of my organization in which I am most comfortable making decisions. Instead,
my role is to be where the greatest *need* is for the organization, and
that may be—and often is—somewhere outside my comfort zone.
For instance, with my marketing background, I feel most comfortable making decisions in that area. However, HFE has a great senior
marketer, and most of my time is needed in other areas. I'm the
CEO, not the head of marketing. And each time I make a leadership decision outside my comfort zone, the efficacy and value of
Socratic leadership and decision making is proved again.

Occasionally I don't follow my own advice, and I step into a
more hands-on decision-making role. This isn't common, and it
usually stems from one of three issues:

- An inexperienced but capable leader needs time to fully
  own his or her area of responsibility; in the meantime,
  I get more involved than I normally would to teach and
  mentor. As that person gains experience, I slowly allow
  more freedom and demonstrate more trust.
- If I find myself getting too involved because I've lost faith
  in a person's judgment or that person is indecisive and
  holding up proper progress, I have to replace that person
  with someone I can trust. In the interim, I may have to
  make more autocratic decisions.
- Sometimes I discover that I'm not willing to let go of a
  decision. If so, I need to discuss the issue with the leader
  in question. I either need to take that decision back—

become the "approver" on the RACI chart—or let that decision be made by others.

Talented people—the kind any leader should want to be surrounded by—don't like to be told what to do. They want to figure things out. I could tell them what I want them to decide, and sometimes I do, but each time I lead autocratically, I risk hindering their development—or worse, losing them over time as they decide to move somewhere they are trusted and loved.

Unselfishness sometimes means letting others lead—consider Peter Herschend. When Jack and Peter's mother and father passed away, Jack and Peter each had 50 percent ownership in HFE and no set transition plan. Yet Peter selflessly came to Jack and suggested that Jack be the CEO and Peter be vice president of marketing, since he believed that is where both skill sets would be maximized. That's being unselfish.

What Makes a Good Leader?

Recently, Google commissioned their internal human resources team to identify and rate the attributes of their best leaders. They were surprised to find that technical knowledge ranked dead last. Instead, attributes like listening well and letting employees make relevant decisions attracted and kept the best people. Google may not realize it, but these are attributes of leading with love.

In today's fast-changing business environment, it is more important to develop pure leadership skills like those described within this book than it is to become a so-called "expert" in a particular area. Economies, knowledge, and required skills change, but the principles of leading with love are timeless and will always benefit any organization.

How can you lead unselfishly? Could you listen better? Are you feeling overwhelmed and hindered from helping anyone? Should you do for one what you wish you could do for everyone? Are you hoarding decisions you should delegate? Being selfless is hard, but as Google discovered, the attributes of leading with love attract and keep the very best.

It all starts tomorrow morning. Whether you begin to take steps to launch a company-wide program like Share It Forward or simply have lunch with someone who needs a listening ear, tomorrow is the day you can start living—and leading with love—selflessly.

Unselfish
Chapter Summary

☑ Unselfish: think of yourself less.

☑ Be unselfish with your personal treasure.
- Define a fixed percentage of your income to give away.
- Ask someone like your tax accountant to hold you accountable.
- Set a finish line so you don't have lifestyle creep.

☑ Be unselfish with your personal time and talent to make yourself, your organization, and the world better.

☑ Help your organization be unselfish.
- Give a fixed percentage of your organization's profits to help those in your organization who are in a personal crisis.
- Give your time and talent to develop internal leaders.
- "Do for one what you wish you could do for everyone."

☑ Be unselfish with your decision-making authority: a strong leader should aim to make as few decisions as possible.

☑ Socratic, rather than autocratic, leading is more effective, because it leads to better decisions and attracts and keeps better talent.

☑ Socratic leading requires:
  • asking more questions
  • facilitating a team discussion with talented people
  • making the best decision possible due to rich discussion
  • summarizing the decision and direction

7

TRUTHFUL
DEFINE REALITY CORPORATELY AND INDIVIDUALLY

The first responsibility of a leader is to
define reality.

Max DePree, chairman emeritus,
Herman Miller

Max DePree was right: one of the most critical jobs of a leader is getting at the truth. Once individuals have the truth, they can deal with it. If not, we can all travel down the wrong path without correction — and the outcome can be treacherous. For leaders to thrive, they must define the truth of the organization's real role in the marketplace and identify its weaknesses and strengths. They must establish how the organization will prevail against the negative forces it will face.

In the same regard, a strong leader assures that the truth is communicated to every individual about his or her performance and how it can be improved. That's why the need for truth is both corporate and individual.

However, identifying and speaking the truth is difficult and sometimes complicated. Individual egos, weak leadership, and conflict avoidance can all lead to an unhealthy organizational culture where truth is not upheld as a key value.

- Have you ever considered the critical distinction between telling corporate and individual truth?
- Do you wish you had usable tools for discovering and communicating truth?
- What can you learn from the last dismissal you handled the wrong way?
- How can you, as a leader, discover the truth about yourself?

7.1

Corporate Truth
on the Table

I took a deep breath and closed my eyes for a moment. What should I do?

I was sitting in our largest conference room with my direct reports and some of their staff. We had recently made a difficult decision to close a money-losing theme park. We took a large financial write-off, which was not good news—no CEO can survive too many of those. Although the previous management had planned and built the park, I still took part of the blame and felt a great deal of pressure. This was a clear failure, and we needed the next step to be a good one.

This meeting was a tense situation where getting at the "corporate truth" would be critical. Corporate truth means dealing with the realities of your specific organization and industry, as contrasted with the truth about an individual. However, as I was learning at that moment, corporate truth can be a slippery fish to land.

Our goal for the meeting was to decide what we would do with this shuttered park and the surrounding acreage. As we discussed the situation, the debate grew rancorous. Nerves frayed as we tried to recommend a course for a board meeting that was only

a month away. Should we tear down the facility? Repurpose it? Sell
it? Build a new attraction to replace it? People began interrupting
one another; voices were rising; faces became red with frustration.

Steps Toward Truth

It was clear we needed some ground rules to gain control of the
discussion and ensure it was constructive and truthful. So, even
as the arguments continued, I stood and walked to the flip chart
we had in the room. I uncapped a thick black marker and wrote
the following rules:

Rule #1: Don't Shoot the Messenger

I said, "You guys need to relax and let the negative opinions come
out. We have to learn from our mistakes so we don't repeat them.
Let's deal with the information, not the person expressing the
opinion." In order for the corporate truth to be uncovered, we
need to remember that no single person is responsible for that
group truth — and we must hear the unfettered individual truth
in order for the corporate truth to be revealed.

Rule #2: Don't Confuse Disagreement
with Conflict

"Healthy disagreement is needed to arrive at the best possible solu-
tion," I said. "Conflict develops when people take the disagreement personally. If we want to get at the corporate truth here, we
have to focus on the disagreement and not on our hurt feelings."

I went on to say that getting the truth on the table was the
first priority, and healthy disagreements were a way to ensure that
would happen. After all, if all of us agreed, some of us weren't
really needed!

Andrew Wexler, our talented chief financial officer, said,
"I agree. At McKinsey we used the phrase 'cuss and discuss' to
assure we got at the truth."

Then Chris Herschend, Peter's son and president of our Ride the Ducks division, chimed in, "Let's make it 'fuss and discuss' — keep it family friendly!" The ensuing laughter broke the ice in the room, and I continued our discussion.

Rule #3: Don't Assume People See It

"We all have different perspectives," I said. "The finance team, creative team, operations team, and marketing team all see the failures of the past and opportunities for the future from a different perspective. Don't assume other people see what you see. Get it out on the table."

To assure this happened, I called on people and made sure everyone in the room spoke, or had a chance to, before we moved to another issue. This approach is especially helpful when the issues are controversial and there is disagreement. Think of the corporate truth as a jigsaw puzzle; without contributions from everyone involved, you will never see the whole picture.

Rule #4: Speak Now or Forever Hold Your Peace

"Before you leave this room, you need to have voiced your opinions. If your opinions are challenged and you lose the argument, you must be reconciled to the rest of this team. You will have your opportunity to persuade the rest of the team to agree with your point of view, but if a vote of your colleagues goes against you — well, you had your chance to speak, so you'll need to get on board with the team. I expect you to support whatever decision we make when you leave this room."

I finished by saying, "I'm going to speak last on each issue so I don't influence the thinking of the team. Don't take that as a lack of energy or passion for the issue. No matter what we think, most people have a hard time expressing a strong opinion that's different than the leaders' opinions. Since we have various levels in the room, let those who are junior to you go first." With that, I put away my Sharpie and sat down to listen.

The discussion went well as we uncovered the various lessons we could learn about what went wrong. However, moving forward, we still had a variety of ideas on the table for the new attraction we would put on this property. As the discussion became more heated, I realized we needed to have clear criteria about our new business decisions for this property.

I pulled out our new-business criteria developed by Rick Todd, our senior vice president of risk management and business administration. I asked Rick to take over the meeting and get input from around the room on how we ranked all of our new-business criteria. Through a steady process of calling on each person, he confirmed that we had the right "nonnegotiable" criteria for this decision, and the team agreed. Then Rick and the team established the right weights and priorities on the "negotiable" criteria for our new-business opportunities.

I have included here the tables Rick and our team came up with, because they can be remarkably helpful tools for organizations trying to get the truth on the table and move forward with a wise decision. If you aren't currently making any team decisions, feel free to skip past these charts.

New Business Criteria: Nonnegotiable

	Concept #1		Concept #2	
Nonnegotiable	Yes	No	Yes	No
1. Supports our vision and mission.				
2. Will be #1 or #2 in its segment.				
3. Possesses a sustainable competitive advantage.				
4. Capable of achieving our agreed upon financial metrics.				
5. We can execute effectively because we have the right people and/or the right partner.				

New Business Criteria: Negotiable

	Weight 1–10	Idea #1		Idea #2	
		Score	Total	Score	Total
1. We have the ability to *exceed* agreed upon financial metrics.	10				
2. We can have best possible location in a large market.	9				
3. It has low recurring capital reinvestment requirements.	7				
4. It is capable of leveraging a well-established brand or working synergistically with one or more of our other businesses.	8				
5. It has distinctive appeal to a large and profitable market segment and is highly repeatable.	10				
6. It is a business that takes advantage of our corporate strength and/or experience.	8				
7. Diversification—It isn't reliant on the same market factors as our current businesses.	5				
8. Up-front cash or debit requirements are within our limit.	6				
9. We can identify a capable and committed champion.	10				
10. The timing of the opportunity and related risk of losing the opportunity are appropriate.	5				
11. The level of HFE independence in opportunity vs. related dependence on third party partner is justified.	8				
Totals					

Weight: Each criteria evaluated for importance and prioritized on a scale of 1–10 (1 being of very little importance).

Scoring: Evaluate each concept against the criteria and assign it a score of 1–5 (1 being low).

Multiply the score times the weight to arrive at the total score for that criteria.

What do all these boxes and numbers have to do with leading with love?

First, getting the truth on the table corporately assures that all voices are heard. If we love our team, it is critical that their talented voices are heard and their opinions considered. I have found that in the heat of the battle, when the numbers are bad or the timing is short, most discussions get truncated; they get emotional, blame is deflected, listening is poor, frustration is high, and all of this often leads to poor thinking or team members who no longer feel trusted. Most people don't leave because of poor performance; they leave because they don't feel valued.

Second, leading with love also means doing the best thing for the organization to protect or add as many jobs as possible for those we care about. Getting the truth on the table assures the best possible decisions are made for the organization's future. Remember, leading with love is never an excuse for being "soft" as a leader. A healthy organization does the most good for the greatest number of people.

Getting the corporate truth isn't easy. Using the robust discussion and decision-making processes noted above takes more time, discipline, and work. However, it engages people at their highest level and leads to the best decisions possible — both outcomes any leader should desire, and both are necessary when leading with love.

7.2

Same as,
More of, Less of

Frank was a superstar. He was the most intuitive leader I had ever worked with in the auto industry. He got to the answer quickly and was usually right. He knew how to solve problems and get things done. He worked tirelessly to make the company better.

However, his hard-driving personality meant that Frank didn't usually vet issues sufficiently or involve those affected by his decisions. Quick decisions are fine when the building is on fire, but Frank had little patience for due process or for hearing other opinions in more routine decisions. This left others discouraged when they didn't feel heard. As the old saying goes, Frank was "occasionally wrong but never in doubt." People on Frank's team appreciated his strengths, but they wished he'd listen and delegate more effectively.

As I sat at my desk late one evening thinking about how best to communicate with Frank what needed to happen, I pulled out an old tool I had used over the years.

Getting at Individual Truth

I wrote out headings on three sections of my paper: "Same as," "More of," and "Less of." In the "Same as" section, I wrote the things I appreciated most about Frank, while I listed the things I would like to see "more of" in the next row. Under "less of," I recorded things that were negative and Frank needed to eliminate or reduce. By putting it in writing, I assured I would crisply communicate both the positive and the negative, as well as be able to review Frank's progress at a later date. This is the actual document I shared with Frank.

Same as:

- Your business judgment is incredible. Your insights into how we can get better are spot-on, and I appreciate your willingness to confront me on what we can do better.
- Your work ethic is endless. You do whatever it takes to get the job done. I cannot express how much that means to me.
- You are proactive. I don't have to tell you. You see it, usually before I do, and are almost always on it by the time I discuss it with you.
- I always trust that you are focused on the right issues to drive improved performance.

More of:

- Play as a team: Set an example of teamwork; use "we" not "they" when discussing the corporate team with the field employees.
- Dialogue together: We need more face-to-face time to dialogue on issues.

Less of:

- Venting to third parties. Address the issue head-on with the person you are frustrated with and keep the frustration more isolated.
- Negative energy. You are a senior leader, and people feed off your energy. Always lead with positive energy and decrease the amount of negative energy you display. Posi-

tive energy and encouragement are contagious, but so is negative energy.

Based on our conversation, Frank agreed to work on the areas discussed. When we sat down six months later, his attitude and behavior were greatly improved, and we both thought the previous discussion and follow-up had proved their worth.

I also asked Frank to go through the same exercise for me so I could learn how to better serve and support Frank as a leader. My publisher wanted me to share this document in the book, but it's *classified*, and if you read it, I'd have to kill you—and I don't want that on my hands!

There are people like Frank in every organization, and they need truthful, direct feedback and follow-up to help them refine their performance and attitude to become fantastic—not just good—leaders.

Team Conflict

Using the Same as/More of/Less of approach can also be effective in a group setting when an entire team is behaving in a dysfunctional manner.

When I first came to Saab, the senior leadership team was rife with conflict and distrust. There was conflict between the original Saab employees (pre-GM acquisition) and the GM transplants, as well as conflict between many of my direct reports. It was a nonfunctioning mess, and there was so little communication taking place I felt the situation warranted an "intervention."

I gathered the team in a hotel conference room with a nice porch and a view of the woods. On that deck we set up eight flip charts, one for each of the eight of us in the exercise. I wrote the name of each individual at the top of one of the charts (including my name) and split the charts into three horizontal sections: Same as, More of, and Less of.

Then I asked each participant to fill in his or her thoughts under each criterion for each person. For instance, I walked to the other seven flip charts and wrote on each chart what I felt that person should do the same, more, and less in the future.

After we'd each done this, I placed eight chairs in a circle for more intimate discussion. Our CFO began, walking up to his chart and going through each point others had written about him to make sure he understood the feedback.

It took nearly four hours to go through all the information, but the discussion was fantastic. We could see that wounds were starting to heal and authentic discussion was beginning to take place again. It was at times very uncomfortable, but it was extremely productive. Speaking the truth isn't always easy, but we can't lead with love unless we love the truth.

The final step that day was to ask each person to summarize a series of action items from their charts on a sheet of paper. I then had each person sign their "contract" as a commitment to how they would behave going forward. We revisited the contracts six and twelve months later and revised them along the way. The team became fired up about the progress we were making, and after a year we were working well together. Disagreements still existed, of course, as they always do—and should! However, the way we were working through conflicts was greatly improved because we had gotten to the corporate and individual truth of the situation.

Leading with love means caring enough about an individual or a team to give and solicit truthful feedback. When leaders provide their teams with the truth about their performance as well as the tools to be successful, *regardless of personal feelings*, this is a sure sign of leading with love.

7.3

The Avoidance

Firing someone is never easy, and it shouldn't be. In a way, it is a death. It is like being shot emotionally, stripped of confidence, and forced into a difficult life situation. Firing someone should be handled with love and care, but it usually isn't. And despite what I know about this, I've made few mistakes more embarrassing and distasteful than when I fired Rex.

Rex was the head of our information technology division at Saab USA. He was energetic and bright. He worked hard and always tried to improve the business. However, he also loved technology for technology's sake and had a "gift" for making simple things complex and missing the essence of an issue. As a result, our five-year IT plan was full of grandiose ideas that went beyond what we needed and didn't address the most pressing issues — not to mention it would cost too much to implement.

When I kept getting complaints from dealers about our systems, I knew I had to make a change. We were losing money and didn't have time to determine whether Rex would always be over his head or if he could improve with development. I decided I didn't have time to talk to Rex about it because "the building was on fire." We had to get things moving in the right direction quickly.

I had a separation agreement prepared for Rex. That's when things got ugly. For some unknown reason, our corporate lawyers in Detroit faxed Rex's separation agreement to the wrong fax number. The person who received the fax read Rex's name on the document and then kindly called our headquarters and got Rex's fax number. Soon after that, Rex watched in shock as his own separation agreement was printed by his fax machine before I'd even sat down with him to tell him he was getting fired.

Nice move.

I was on the phone with a customer when Rex stormed into my office.

"What in the heck is this?" he screamed at me.

"Rex, settle down and give me a second," I said calmly.

He didn't back down. "No, you give *me* a second right now!" His face burned with anger.

I sat down with Rex and saw the separation agreement in his hand and said, "I don't know how you got this, but I am sorry it happened this way." What ensued was an incredibly tense and difficult conversation. My feelings of embarrassment and regret have never faded. I felt horrible about how I handled the whole situation. Regardless of the fax mix-up, I hadn't conveyed to Rex the truth about his performance along the way or worked with him to improve it, and then I'd failed to fire him respectfully.

A few years later, I saw Rex in a grocery store, but he didn't see me. I moved in the opposite direction to avoid any contact.

I felt like a jerk. I probably was.

Experience Applied

About fifteen years, a few gray hairs, and several mistakes later, I juxtapose how I botched Rex's firing with how we handled a recent situation at HFE. We needed to let a senior executive named Carl go, but we handled it much better than Rex's dismissal. What I learned from firing Carl could be a good lesson for all leaders in how to lead with love: relieving a person of a job by speaking the truth *and* protecting that person's dignity at the same time.

Here's what I learned:

Ensure that the employee understands how serious the issues are before firing is an option.

I had a single conversation with Rex about his performance—and that wasn't until his awkward dismissal! Rex didn't know in advance about the problems we had with his performance. I should have confronted Rex as soon as I recognized the problems his performance was causing, but I didn't.

On the other hand, we had three or four discussions with Carl about his performance issues at HFE. He wasn't happy to hear about it, but he was not surprised when we finally offered him a severance package.

Clearly this rule applies to underperforming employees, not to cases where there has been some kind of impropriety or other serious offense that requires instant action.

Handle the tough day in a dignified manner.

Rex's dismissal was not dignified; he was screaming and I was trying to settle him down. He left that day and never came back in the office. To the contrary, Carl's departure from HFE was as smooth and friendly as possible. Unless there has been an impropriety, we typically try to avoid escorting people out of the office upon dismissal. We balance this process with appropriate protection for the company and its assets, but with that protection in place, I would much rather allow separated employees to leave relatively seamlessly instead of embarrassing them with an unnecessary escort out the door.

Help the dismissed person get his or her life back on track.

Rex signed his separation agreement and stormed out the door, making any offer of transition help very difficult, and I didn't see him again until the supermarket encounter. But with Carl, I was aggressive in offering assistance. I sat down with him to explain how I thought he could learn from his experience at HFE and do better in his next job. I focused on his strengths as well as his weaknesses. He subsequently landed a very good job with a great company.

Be gracious.

Being gracious in difficult times is part of leading with love. HFE is typically kind and gracious in dealing with employees who are terminated, and we use a variety of tools to help with the transition: if a job is being eliminated, we try to provide adequate notice to allow time to find a job while still employed, severance, and/or outplacement counseling services if justified. The point is that we would rather err on the side of being gracious—and I know my father would agree.

Have you ever had to fire someone? If you're a leader and you haven't, you will! Be sure to handle the dismissal with truth and integrity, in a way that allows you to look yourself in the mirror the next day and like what you see. Make sure when you see the person you dismissed in a grocery store, you don't have to run in the other direction. I wonder, *If it were more painful for corporate America to let employees go, both financially and emotionally, would companies be more hesitant to engage that tactic?*

Just recently I saw Carl in church, and he came right up to me with a big smile, said hello, and shook my hand. I asked him how his new job was, and he said, "Great!"

That's all I needed to hear. It told me that I had done a better job this time around of leading with love and valuing truth.

7.4

The Truth Will
Set You Free

What happens when *you* are the one who needs to hear the truth?

Leadership is a lonely business. When we rely only on our own perspective, we miss our blind spots. We do the best we can, but if we have nobody telling us the real truth, we will not improve over time.

The unfortunate news is that the more senior you are in your organization, the more difficult it is to get the truth about how you're performing. Finding someone you can trust to give you honest feedback is a rare gift that all leaders need but few receive.

You will have to find these companions on your own. Your trusted confidants may come from your organization or from your personal life; either way, the undeniable fact is they need to tell you the truth about who you are and where you need to grow. They need to confront you when you are wrong and watch for patterns of poor behavior and negative patterns in your decision making. Preferably, these "truth tellers" are not impacted by your decisions, so you can be assured there is no ulterior motive. I found my most trusted "truth tellers" in an unlikely place: a Bible study at Harvard Business School.

Harvard Business School (HBS) isn't for the faint of heart. About 10,000 overachievers apply for the 800 slots a year. Each class has a 10 percent forced curve, so no matter how competent you are, if 90 of 100 others do better than you, you "earn" what is called a "low pass" and fail the course. With two low passes in the first year, you "hit the screen" and are asked to leave the school. And people wonder why HBS graduates are so aggressive!

Growing up on farmland in Battle Creek, Michigan, and graduating from a small liberal arts college whose mascot is a "Briton" (don't ask!) didn't arm me with the confidence needed to engage with the Goldman Sachs boys who lived in New York City.

In fact, I was so intimidated during the first day of class that I froze during the introductions. The person next to me was rocket-scientist smart; two chairs down was a guy who had just worked on the largest merger in corporate history. I didn't think my plant foreman experience watching people get drunk and sleep in boxes was going to excite anyone, so I reacted quickly and decided to reference my stellar sports career instead: "My name is Joel Manby" — long pause — "and my claim to fame ... is I guarded Magic Johnson in a high school basketball game" — nervous laughter — "and I held him to 42 points."

The class burst out laughing, and so began my HBS career in "acting." Thereafter, I regularly put on humorous skits for the class along with David Lopez and Leslie Goldberg (now Leslie Gold, the top female DJ in New York City!). I also starred in the B School Musical, a tradition at HBS. I needed such diversions, because my first year was brutal. Half our grade was based on class participation, but at first I was too nervous to speak. I was struggling emotionally and was homesick as well.

However, I attended a Christian Fellowship meeting and met three men there: Vaughn Brock, Dougal Cameron, and Kevin Jenkins. We started a Bible study together and met every Wednesday morning. Over time we became close friends. In fact, this ring of friendship has proven to be one of the smartest decisions I have made in my life.

My lifelong accountability group: Vaughn Brock,
Dougal Cameron, me, and Kevin Jenkins.

The group proved to be a great sounding board for me. These
men had great wisdom and were among the very best people I
had ever met on this earth. They advised me on dating, marriage,
career, temptations, investing—you name it, these guys seemed
to be able to help. Most importantly, I knew they would tell me
the truth, the whole truth, and nothing but the truth—and I
needed that.

Upon graduation, we committed to stay close. We instituted a
monthly call, an annual golf trip, and an every-other-year vacation
with our families. Although the golf and family vacations haven't
always been on time, you can set your clock to our monthly calls:
the first Friday of every month at 10:00 a.m. Eastern time. So
don't call me then, because I'll be on the phone.

To this day, nearly thirty years later, I love this call. I get the
truth, and I speak the truth to them—the truth about how we
really feel inside. We speak the truth about our fears, our frustra-
tions, our marriages, and our careers. We even call one another's
wives occasionally to make sure we are telling one another the
truth. During a time when one of us was really struggling in our
marriage, one of us called our accountability partner's wife just
to see if we were getting a balanced story. We still didn't feel as if

we were getting both sides of the story, so two of us flew to the other's home so we could meet with them face-to-face and help build back their relationship.

We have helped each other through sorrow and loneliness, through success and failure. These are men I would die for. And that's why we can speak the truth to one another. There is almost no greater gift in life than honest friends, and all leaders need to hear the truth about who they are and the nature of their strengths and weaknesses.

You may be thinking, *What's all this about marriage and fears and accountability—I thought this was a leadership book!* I understand that concern, but I submit that if someone knows you well enough to confront you with the truth about key decisions you make, that person is the kind of friend who can guide you in *all* areas of life, including leadership.

Character is the root of a leader's success—and only our very closest friends can hold us accountable to the character we strive for and require to be quality leaders over time. Only our closest friends will see the weaknesses in our long-term patterns of behavior. Only real "truth tellers" will know if we are leading with love at home and at work. Having someone at work who will tell you when you screw up in a meeting is a gift—but a friend who knows you for a lifetime and will really confront you is a treasure of immense value.

What about you? Who can tell you the real truth and hold you accountable to your commitments? Do you have anyone who really knows you? If not, this may be the best advice you get from this book. It takes dedication and time to make this happen, but it's worth it. Leading with love begins with an honest assessment of yourself, and self is the one person you can never be absolutely honest with.

Getting to the truth corporately and individually is difficult, but you now have tools to help you do exactly that. Whether you are finding the truth or communicating it to others, being a "truth teller" is an absolute requirement for leading with love.

Truthful
Chapter Summary

☑ Truthful: define reality corporately and individually.

☑ Be truthful about the organization.
- Don't "shoot the messenger" or confuse disagreement with conflict.
- Don't assume people see the truth — speak up.
- As a leader, it's usually best to speak last.
- Consider using a decision-making matrix in more complex organizational decisions.

☑ Be truthful to an employee.
- Same as/More of/Less of is an effective tool to communicate the truth.
- The same technique can be used in a larger group.
- Getting at the truth keeps the best people and creates the best decisions.

☑ Be truthful in a dismissal.
- It should not be a surprise to the person being dismissed.
- Handle the tough day in a dignified manner.
- Be proactive in giving the person you are firing advice and helping that person get his or her life back on track.

- Be gracious. Letting somebody go shouldn't be effortless so that you do it less often.

☑ Be open to hearing the truth.
  - No matter how you do it, find an accountability partner or partners in your life who will always tell you the truth about yourself.
  - Don't guard Magic Johnson in a high school basketball game!

8

FORGIVING
RELEASE THE GRIP
OF THE GRUDGE

The longer you hold a grudge, the longer
the grudge has a hold on you.
Jeff Henderson, Buckhead Church

Has anyone ever done you wrong? Forgiving is very difficult, I know. Whether or not you were able to forgive has probably shaped you in one way or another.

Here's the issue: you may have been wronged and deserve to hold a grudge. But the real question is, what purpose does it serve? Is holding a grudge effective?

We love to imagine exactly how we would tell off the person who wronged us or dream about how we might take revenge. Holding a grudge can feel good, and we all have a story of being wronged that seems to justify our grudge.

But what was done to us doesn't matter in the end — all that matters is how we respond.

- Have you ever forgiven someone who has wronged your organization and seen redemption?
- Have you ever forgiven someone who has wronged your organization and regretted it when that person reoffended? When should you draw the line?
- Have you ever witnessed the positive ripple effect forgiveness can have, even beyond your power to comprehend?
- Do you ever feel trapped and limited by the grudges you hold?

8.1

Eric

Eric is a very bright eighteen-year-old who worked as a seasonal employee at our Stone Mountain Park attraction in Atlanta. The oldest of seven brothers and sisters, he has never had a permanent father figure in his life, so all of the money Eric earns goes right back to his family.

One day last year, Eric was terminated for violating company policy. I had met Eric once but didn't know him and was unaware that he had been released.

A week or so later, I received a message from Eric through Facebook. He apologized for what he had done and asked if I would consider giving him another chance. I wouldn't normally get involved in an issue like that, but I was impressed with Eric's tone. He was contrite, and he admitted he had made a mistake and was sorry for it. In addition, I was impressed with what I saw in the rest of Eric's Facebook profile; he seemed like a humble and decent young man.

I emailed our general manager and the head of human resources at Stone Mountain, Gerald and Michael, and asked that Eric's file be reviewed. I made it clear I was not asking that Eric be rehired — simply that his dismissal be reevaluated based on Eric's heartfelt request.

Forgiving Someone Who Has Wronged the Organization

Gerald and Michael decided to give Eric another chance after he passed all tests regarding knowledge of our policies and procedures.

About a month after Eric rejoined Stone Mountain Park, I called Gerald to see if he would invite Eric to an Atlanta Braves baseball game, and the two of them could be my guests. Gerald checked his schedule and replied, "Joel, I will check with Eric, but he is scheduled to work that day, and I know that he will not want to take the time off. He really wants the hours, because his family needs his financial help." Gerald was correct; Eric worked instead.

I continued to reach out to Eric occasionally via Facebook. My heart went out to an eighteen-year-old who wouldn't take time away from work because he was trying to keep his family above water financially. That was humbling and reminded me of my dad's work ethic.

The next spring, about six months after Eric contacted me on Facebook, I was walking through Stone Mountain Park and ran into Eric. He looked happy and full of energy. I said, "Hey, Eric, great to see you. How ya doing?"

He replied, "Mr. Manby, I . . . um . . . I am doing just fine, sir. Hey, I was . . . um . . . I was wondering if you might be willing to come to my high school graduation."

My world seemed to stop as I absorbed his question. Scenes of my entire experience with Eric flashed through my mind—his dismissal, his Facebook message, his request for another chance, his work ethic, his efforts to support his family, his ability to overcome obstacles. I thought I was an insignificant influence in his life, yet he was asking *me* to attend his graduation. I felt my throat tighten, and tears welled up in my eyes. I couldn't get any words out.

I fumbled for my smart phone in an effort to look away from Eric, but I could hardly read the screen through my tears. My emotions surprised me, but I managed to get the words out: "Um, let me check my schedule here."

I gathered myself, wiped away the tears, and found the date: May 21. Amazingly, I had just that day canceled a commitment for the same weekend. "Eric," I said, looking up at him, "I would be honored to be there. Thanks for asking me."

"Thanks," he said, smiling.

As his broad six-feet-four-inch frame walked away, I felt so proud of Gerald and Michael. They had given Eric another chance, and a fine young man who had the odds stacked against him was able to succeed.

Eric finished his senior year in high school and got a letter of recommendation for the naval academy from a US senator. Although he was not accepted to the academy, we were told the biggest reason was his lack of extracurricular activities — but that was because Eric was always working to support his family! Life isn't always fair.

On May 21, Gerald and I attended Eric's graduation. After the ceremony, I had a wonderful time meeting Eric's mother and

The positive ripples of forgiveness:
Eric with his mother and six siblings and Joel.

all of his siblings. I told Eric how proud I was of him, and after we took a few pictures, Gerald and I left him alone to be with his family. Eric enlisted with the army, and he will get his college education through military assistance programs.

Choosing to Forgive

How does a leader know when to forgive someone? When do you rehire an employee who was released but wants another chance? What happens if you give someone a second chance and that person messes up even worse? We don't have a set formula at Herschend Family Entertainment, but we encourage our leaders to use a set of questions to help them make the right decision:

- *Is this a one-time offense or a recurring theme?* What is the person's track record and reputation? Was this offense inconsistent with everything else we have witnessed concerning this person's character and reputation?
- *What is the person's self-awareness of his or her shortcoming?* Does this person have a contrite heart about the offense? Did he or she apologize? Do I really believe the offense won't happen again?
- *How does the person's direct manager feel?* We always try to let the person's direct manager make the decision, even if the appeal comes to a senior leader. The direct manager is closest to the action, and we should never force that manager to take someone he or she doesn't want. At times, however, there are extenuating circumstances that break this rule.
- *Give the offender the benefit of the doubt if you're not sure,* giving him or her another chance to make it right.

When I was a new board member at HFE and Jack Herschend was still chairman of the company, the board seemed disappointed with Jack because he was not moving fast enough to replace people who were not hitting their numbers.

Jack said in a very calm but very stern voice, "I would rather be known for moving too slow than moving too fast."

Wise words from a wise man. Because of Jack's example, I would also rather be known for being slow to fire and quick to forgive instead of being quick to fire and slow to forgive. Not every leader agrees with these words, but if you're still reading, I suspect you're a leader who deeply desires to transform the way your organization functions. Leading with love, even if it means giving undeserved second chances, is the right way to build an organization for long-term health.

Second Chances Don't Always Have a Happy Ending

I know what some of you are thinking: *Joel hasn't seen my situation!*

Perhaps not, but I have lived through enough difficult second-chance scenarios to know they don't always end well. That doesn't mean, however, that we shouldn't give second chances.

I have led multiple team members who were alcoholics or drug addicts or suffered from mental illness. One—we'll call her Betty—was a senior executive with a stellar track record who started showing signs of inconsistency. Betty started leaving early from work, not acting like herself in meetings, and displaying strange behavior on phone calls. Next came a DUI. Then a separation from her husband. After that, rehab. The company paid for her rehab program—an expensive thirty-day treatment—and held her job open.

She came back stronger, and her performance improved. However, it didn't last. She went in and out of rehab a few more times, resulting in her being demoted to a lesser but still senior role. Betty's performance was not as productive as in the past, and the pattern of exiting and reentering rehab didn't show signs of changing.

I struggled with the decision. Although she no longer reported to me in her new role, I felt I needed to be the one who made the call. It wasn't fair to her new boss to force that decision on him. I sought counsel from longtime executives who understood the culture of the company. After Betty had a few more additional stints in rehab, I finally decided to give her a severance package.

The story didn't end well. Betty never shook her dependence on alcohol, and she died at the age of fifty-eight. Her funeral was incredibly sad.

In hindsight, I don't regret the second and third and sixth chances we gave Betty. She made her own choices, and no leader can truly control what an employee chooses. But what a leader can control is his or her own actions. In Betty's case, we acted honorably and truthfully.

Forgiveness is sometimes agonizing, and it doesn't always lead to a happy ending. I am not suggesting that we toss out our organizational standards and goals—simply that we keep our hearts soft enough to be open to forgiveness. It may not always be the easiest thing to do, but it's always the right thing.

For Eric, forgiveness did end well; giving him a second chance was a small pebble in a pond. The ripples fanned out from our decision to rehire him. Eric was able to support his family, finish high school, and serve in the army. And soon after he will attend college. Who knows how far the ripples from that act of forgiveness will continue to spread?

The next chapter affirms that indeed the ripples can continue for years—even across multiple generations!

8.2

Marilou McCully

Marilou McCully was Marki's aunt—and a very special woman who taught me more about the power of forgiveness than any other person in my life. She exemplified that one act of forgiveness can ripple across hundreds or thousands of lives across multiple generations.

Marilou Hobolth married Ed McCully in June 1951. Both loved God, loved each other, and looked forward to a wonderful life together. Ed was a talented man with a bright future. He graduated from Wheaton College in 1949 near the top of his class, the senior class president, and a national Hearst Corporation debating champion.

After one year of law school, he decided, along with some close friends and their wives, to move to Ecuador as missionaries. They planned to live among the Waodani, an isolated, hostile tribe deep in the rain forest.

In order to reach the Waodani, the young missionaries would need to earn their trust. They began flying over the jungle regularly, even dropping gifts from the airplane, and the Waodani reciprocated by placing gifts in a basket suspended in one spot from the tight circling plane.

After months of friendly air-to-land contact, the five men flew the bright yellow plane into the jungle and landed on a small strip

The ripple effect of forgiveness is still spreading sixty years after Ed's death. Ed and Marilou McCully, 1951.

of sandy beach. They set up camp at "Palm Beach" on Tuesday, January 3, 1956.

On Friday, after three days without seeing anyone else, the missionaries spotted a Waodani man and two Waodani women calmly walking out of the jungle. The interaction lasted for a few hours as the men did their best to communicate without a common language. The Waodani seemed to be in good spirits when they left.

On Sunday, things changed. As he was flying the plane back into the jungle, one of the missionaries — Nate Saint — spotted a group of ten Waodani headed toward Palm Beach. Just past noon, Nate radioed his wife, Marge, and said: "Looks like the Waodani will be here for the early afternoon service. Pray for us. This is the day. Will contact you next at 4:30."

The missionaries, including Aunt Marilou's husband, Ed, were never seen alive again. All five of the young men died on the points of Waodani spears.

But that's not where the story ends.

Ripples

The men left behind five wives and nine children, and news of their deaths was quickly broadcast around the world and on the front page of *LIFE* magazine. Many people questioned why the men had gone in the first place, while many others called for revenge on the Waodani. There was ample confusion and debate.

For the wives, however, everything was clear. They all chose to forgive the Waodani, powerfully demonstrating that love is really a verb.

I asked Marilou how she could possibly forgive the people who had murdered her husband. She nearly dismissed the question, saying, "That's what God would ask us to do, and it's what God did for us. Besides, being bitter wasn't going to help me, and it wasn't going to bring Ed back." Instead of giving in to hate and despair, the wives chose to follow the ripple of their husbands' loving example.

The ripple wasn't done spreading.

Six months after the murders, Elisabeth Elliot (the wife of Jim Elliot, one of the missionaries) and Rachel Saint (Nate's sister) befriended a Waodani woman named Dayuma who had fled the tribe. Together they decided to return to the jungle to complete the work the men had started.

Can you imagine?

Yet Rachel and Elisabeth, along with her young daughter, Valerie, moved into the jungle to live with the Waodani. The women not only survived among the Waodani, but they helped transform the culture of violence into a culture of love and respect. Before their arrival, anthropologists who studied the Waodani described them as the most violent people group they had ever seen. They were killing themselves off and heading toward extinction.

But then the ripple spread: love and forgiveness are a better way to live. The Waodani began to change their way of life, choosing peace instead of violence. It was later learned that the five missionaries had a gun during the attack and did not use it on the Waodani but instead fired it into the air in an attempt to scare off the attackers. Marilou told Marki and me, "Our husbands discussed whether or not they would use their guns on the

Waodani and decided not to. They felt that they all were ready for heaven, but the Waodani were not."

Sometimes leading with love takes an amazing amount of courage!

Rachel spent the rest of her life with the tribe, dying of cancer at the age of eighty, and still the ripple effect of forgiveness continues to this day. Marki has taken two of our daughters, Ryn and Erinn, to live for a week with the Waodani in the jungle in Ecuador, along with members of the five men's extended families. On that trip, Marki and the girls befriended a man named Mincaye, one of the ten Waodani warriors in the killing party. He had become a changed man.

Later Mincaye made a trip to the United States. He and Steve Saint joined Steven Curtis Chapman, a contemporary Christian recording artist, on tour to tell this amazing story. While in the states, Mincaye also attended the graduation of Jesse Saint, Nate Saint's grandson. Why? Because Mincaye is Jesse's godfather and had baptized Jesse in the same river where he helped kill Jesse's grandfather about forty years before.

There was no good to be seen in this tragedy at the time those five men were killed in 1956. However, now we can see that an

The ripple continues. Marki with Mincaye;
his wife, Umpora; and our daughter Erinn.

entire tribe was changed forever and turned from hatred toward love.

The ripple effect of forgiveness is powerful.

Just think of how history could have been different. What if the women had held a grudge—nobody would have blamed them! They had a right to be bitter, and they had a right to immediately flee Ecuador. But if they had, they would have been stripped of the opportunity to help transform this tribe's future.

Forgiving Someone Who Wrongs You

I remember clearly when Marki first told me this story. I thought, "This can't be true. *Nobody* would go back into the jungle to minister to a savage tribe that had just killed their spouses. Who could forgive in *that* situation?"

When I'd spent sufficient time with Marilou, however, I could see she was a rare person. She was gentle and kind but tough as nails at the same time. She was a woman at peace with herself and with God. She lived with no resentment and had chosen a life of forgiveness.

Chosen is a key word. Marilou's life story demonstrates that it isn't about what has *happened* to us so much as it is about how we *react*. Her forgiveness was indeed a choice, just as agape love is a choice.

In one sense, this story seems impossible to relate to—what do the decisions of a handful of women fifty years ago in an Ecuadorian jungle have to do with leading a modern organization? But once we understand that forgiveness can cause unimaginably positive transformation, we see how essential these women's model is for the leaders of today.

Transforming an Organization

Let's face it: as leaders we have many opportunities either to hold a grudge or to forgive. The choice is ours to make. I'm not pretending for one minute that forgiveness is easy. The opposite is true — just as leading with love is not easy. It takes work and is sometimes counterintuitive.

When we choose to forgive others, however, it releases our anger and allows a deep wound to heal. Bearing a grudge keeps the wound open, and although we don't always realize it, we are the ones who are harmed, rather than those who harmed us. If we don't forgive, anger lives in us, and angry leaders create fear in an organization. That can lead employees to avoid risk and please the angry boss at all costs. This will not maximize any organization. Forgiveness releases you, not the person you are forgiving.

It's like the Malacy McCourt quote: "Resentment is like taking poison and waiting for the other person to die." A lack of forgiveness makes us an unattractive person, and we can lose respect as a leader. Have you ever gone to a class reunion and talked to an old classmate who is stuck in life? An incident occurred that they cannot forget, and since they cannot forgive, their life remains forever stuck in the same spot. They are still angry and unable to move forward.

I think Jeff Henderson, pastor of Buckhead Church, is right: we need to "release the grip of the grudge." Forgiveness is not easy, and it doesn't always turn out as planned, but it's always the right thing to do. My friend Eric at our Stone Mountain Park was given another chance, and now his life is on track. Who knows how his life would have turned out without a job? And now, who knows how many lives he might change for the better, or how many people he will forgive?

An act of forgiveness is a pebble in the pond, and the ripples can continue far beyond our ability to know. To a leader who is leading with love, this sounds like a wonderful promise. Is there someone you need to forgive?

Forgiving
Chapter Summary

☑ Forgiving: release the grip of the grudge.

☑ What was done to you doesn't matter in the
end — all that matters is how you respond.

☑ Forgive those who have wronged your
organization.
  • Consider giving them another chance if it is
    a one-time offense, they are aware of their
    shortcomings, and they want to improve, or if
    you have any doubt about letting them go.
  • Be slow to fire and quick to forgive.
  • Forgiving someone and offering a second
    chance doesn't always work out well, but con-
    sider it anyway.

☑ Forgive someone who has wronged you.
  • The longer you hold a grudge, the longer the
    grudge has a hold on you.
  • Forgiveness releases you to focus on love and
    relationship, not anger.
  • Forgiveness can release the person you for-
    give and give that person a fresh start.
  • Forgiveness has a positive ripple effect that
    often extends far beyond our comprehension.

9

DEDICATED
STICK TO YOUR VALUES
IN ALL CIRCUMSTANCES

I am in love with hope.

Mitch Albom, author of
Tuesdays with Morrie

One of the primary roles of a leader is to give hope. This can be done in a variety of ways but is consistently achieved when clarity of vision, mission, and values is coupled with strong financial success. A leader needs to clearly communicate how the organization will win in a competitive marketplace and then execute that plan. Employees feel hopeful and free when they know what is expected, what to deliver, and where the organization is headed.

Leading with that kind of love requires dedication.

But the payoff is huge: such dedicated love will create hope and enthusiasm in the organization. Leading with love needs to be taught and measured; we need to care *how* people achieve their tasks, not only *if* they achieve them. Leading with love needs to be integrated into an organization's operating model, but we must still *lead*, using our power and love while navigating difficult decisions and difficult times with unwavering dedication.

- How do we lead with love while properly using the power we have as leaders?
- Can love and power really coexist — and if so, where is that modeled?
- How can leading with love be integrated into the operating model of an organization, and how can it be measured and tracked?
- Are there strategies for being dedicated to leading with love even when times and decisions are tough?

9.1

Dedication to Love

———

Two millennia ago an itinerant Jewish preacher named Jesus of Nazareth called his friends together for a dinner. This wasn't like the normal meals that group enjoyed, however—Jesus knew it was his last meal. The next day he would be executed by the Roman government. So on that final night, Jesus had to decide how to summarize his teachings so that his twelve followers could carry on his message.

Think of all the options before him. He could have:

1. given them a written scroll that summarized all his teachings,
2. given them money to expand their ministry,
3. given them divine powers to make believers of the skeptics, or
4. introduced them to leaders who would have political influence.

I know I would have done something like that—especially if option 3 was within my grasp! However, he surprised his friends with something so unexpected that it echoed through the ages, changing even the way organizations in twenty-first-century America are led.

As his friend John later remembered, Jesus "got up from the meal, took off his outer clothing, and wrapped a towel around his waist. After that, he poured water into a basin and began to wash his disciples' feet, drying them with the towel that was wrapped around him" (John 13:4–5).

Using Love and Power

In the culture of ancient Palestine, such a gesture was considered the ultimate in self-effacement and humility—bordering on humiliation! Only slaves washed other people's feet. And given that most of the twelve disciples were gaining conviction about the divinity of their leader, Jesus' actions struck them as all the more extraordinary.

Peter, the most outspoken of Jesus' friends, was not pleased by what was happening. He said, "Lord, are you going to wash my feet?"

Jesus must have seen the confusion in those familiar eyes, because he replied, "You do not realize now what I am doing, but later you will understand."

"No," said Peter, "you shall never wash my feet."

Peter wasn't easily dissuaded—I've had more than a few people like him working for me!

But something bigger was happening than a mere argument about whether Jesus was acting like a slave—he was showing his friends a completely new way of leading. So he answered, "Unless I wash you, you have no part with me" (John: 13:6–8).

The fact that Jesus chose to embody his leadership on the night before his death by washing his "employees'" feet represents a compelling example for every leader who has followed him. The occasion seared the importance of serving into the minds of his disciples and challenged all who came after him to consider that leading with love might really be the best way to change the world.

Dedicated to Love

If you lead anything or anyone, you are in a position of power, and if you lead with love, you will surprise others—just like Jesus surprised Peter. I am not suggesting that any of us is like Jesus, but I am suggesting that all of us have the opportunity to abuse our power or to use it well. To hoard it or give it away.

In my experience before Herschend Family Entertainment, most people who had any type of leadership role *focused* on power: how to accumulate it, how to wield it, how to hold on to it. They had no intention of giving power away. No intention, in other words, of leading with love. After all, doesn't the notion of showing love toward employees mean a leader is soft and weak?

As I have said before, as leaders we all have to use the power given us to get things done: to set aggressive targets, to hold others accountable, to ask for resources, to make tough decisions, and to rally people to a common goal and get results. If our organizations go belly-up, what good is love?

Great leaders, however, do all of those things and also understand how to lead with and incorporate love simultaneously. It isn't easy or intuitive, which is why it requires a lifetime of dedication.

Martin Luther King Jr. understood this well. In his 1967 annual report delivered at the eleventh convention of the Southern Christian Leadership Conference in Atlanta, the civil rights icon said, "Power without love is reckless and abusive, and love without power is sentimental and anemic." Dr. King, arguably one of the greatest leaders of all time, understood that love and power must be harnessed together to get the most important things done.

Adam Kahane, author of *Power and Love*, writes about the need for leaders to integrate love and power:

> A system that follows only the impulses of compassion and solidarity [love] will lose its competitiveness; a system that follows only the impulses of resolve and purposefulness [power] will sacrifice its people needlessly and risk its capability for growth and recovery. A

mix of power and love, however, becomes a stance that a leader can hold, and this stance may, in the end, be the single most important factor in enabling a leader to accomplish great things.*

Why is it, then, that nearly three-quarters of all leaders have a very difficult time using both power and love, especially under stress? They tend to revert to the side they are most comfortable with and *ignore* the other. We have all worked with leaders who scoff at anything that has to do with core values or virtues. They think this very idea is soft and gets in the way of profits; talking about love should be relegated to the home, they say.

They are as wrong as it is possible to be.

Unfortunately, most organizations — from businesses to political systems — have been influenced by such thinking and are characterized by an excess of power and a dearth of love.

At HFE we think Jesus' example of leading with love by washing the feet of his friends is a powerful and poignant reminder that love really can change the world. Love works, even when it seems counterintuitive or even upside down. That's why any of our employees who completes our Leading with Love training course has the option to receive a sculpture of Jesus washing Peter's feet. This isn't about religion — some Christian employees choose not to receive the sculpture, while employees of other faiths or no faith at all cherish it. At HFE we focus on successful behaviors, not particular beliefs. The sculpture is simply a physical reminder of a truth that can transform any organization: that the *use* of power need not become the *abuse* of power.

Given the triumph of power over love in most organizations, leaders have to be *dedicated* to leading with love. Leading with love puts leaders in profoundly different roles than they're used to — sometimes uncomfortable roles. If you choose to lead with

---

*Adam Kahane, *Power and Love* (San Francisco: Berrett-Koehler, 2010): quoted in Art Kleiner, "How to Balance Power and Love," *Strategy and Business,* 7 March 2011.

love, others around you may not "get" what you're doing. Do it anyway. Leading with love is more important than the temporary approval of your coworkers. Choosing to lead with love is the single most difficult decision a leader can make, but a wise leader dedicates himself or herself to it because it is also the single best way to lead an organization.

The path can be lonely. Some, who have never known any other way but to fight, claw, and scratch, will not understand. Love them anyway.

Some need to admonish publicly. Be patient anyway.

Some cannot encourage others. Be kind to them anyway.

Some have been burned and do not trust anyone. Be trusting anyway.

Some are selfish, thinking only of themselves. Be unselfish anyway.

Some don't always tell the whole truth. Be truthful anyway.

Some will hold a grudge and choose anger. Be forgiving anyway.

Some may not be dedicated to leading with love. Be dedicated anyway.

What will you choose to do?

"Divine Servant"® is the copyrighted and trade-marked creation of Christian artist Max Greiner Jr. of Kerrville, Texas © (www.maxgreinerart.com).

9.2

Be versus Do

If we are dedicated to leading with love, it is critical to integrate love into our operating model so our teams see it in action and witness its successes. Many organizations talk about values, but few truly integrate those values into how leaders are evaluated and chosen and how organizational results are measured.

I recently gained insight into this issue when I heard Andy Stanley give a talk on *be* goals versus *do* goals. Andy's premise is that most people create many *do* goals in life: have a certain career, reach a certain income level, have a certain net worth, build a certain size family, and so on. And we all have *way* too many to-do lists!

However, a *do* goal can't define *how* we will get there. What set of values will guide our decisions? Is it okay to be dishonest? Is it okay to be focused exclusively on our interests before considering the impact on others? What about exploiting others in order to achieve our goals? Are our marriage and family going to come first? Or does success come before family? Do the ends justify the means? *Do* goals may be good, but they are not enough.

In addition to having *do* goals, it's critical to define the values that will drive our lives. These are what Andy calls our *be* goals. What kind of person do we want to be? What values will we uphold? What kind of integrity will we have when nobody is watching? How do we want to treat others regardless of how they treat us?

We all have to-do lists, but how many of us have to-be lists?

Most people don't—and the same is true for organizations.

Integrating Love into an Organization

All organizations clearly define their *do* goals. What is their mission? What kind of guest experience do they want? What is their profit goal? Their cash flow goal? Even nonprofits have specific metrics for success, even if they aren't specifically financial.

In that regard, Herschend Family Entertainment is no different. We have a clearly established business model revolving around our *do* goals. We have metrics of success for the customer experience, employee satisfaction, safety results, brand definition, and financial results. In other words, we clearly define *what* we do every day to earn a profit. Our business model is expressed at a very high level in the arrow diagram below.

What makes us different from most organizations is that we also clearly define our *be* goals through leading with love. This is the fletching of the arrow in our diagram—the part of the arrow that guides its flight and ensures its aim is true. What

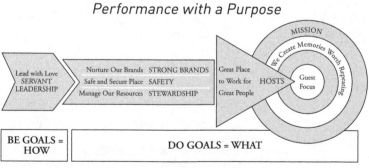

Performance with a Purpose

kind of leaders does HFE want? What behaviors and attitudes are expected? How will they balance love with their *do* goals? In other words, *how* do we want our leaders to treat each other and our employees while achieving the expected financial results?

Do goals will constantly change over time, while *be* goals should be timeless and rarely, if ever, change. *Be* goals represent the heart and soul of an organization, its culture. And we put our money where our mouth is. All leaders at HFE are measured on both the *do* goals and the *be* goals during their annual review. We use the popular tool called the 2 x 2 matrix to assure that we capture both the numeric performance *and* how the leader achieves results.

If a leader scores high on his or her goal achievement (to do) as well as leading with love (to be), the leader will get the best raise — and if he or she does poorly at both, that leader should expect a pink slip soon! Leaders who do well in only one area

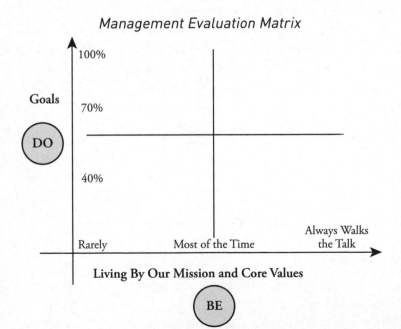

Management Evaluation Matrix

are given tools and training to help them succeed in their area of weakness, and all senior leaders in the company must excel in both areas.

Typically, people who work for me score themselves lower than I score them on leading with love, so most of the time our conversations are positive and encouraging. In fact, most of the difficult discussions surround the inability to hit financial targets. This indicates to me how well leading with love is consistently followed at HFE.

Leaders and employees understand the difference between *do* and *be* goals—and they appreciate any organization that can unite them. As Jack reminded us in chapter 2, this tension between doing and being is to be *embraced*, not *eliminated*. It is only when a leader learns how to manage that tension—a process that takes dedication—that a leader is truly leading with love.

Leading with Love
in Tough Times

The Great Recession that started in 2008 caused almost every organization in the country to make very difficult decisions regarding budgets, staff, and ongoing obligations. Herschend Family Entertainment was no different.

In chapter 4, I mentioned the encouraging note I got from Jack that lifted me during this recession. Yet there were a number of additional actions by the HFE team that were humbling and inspiring and showed unending dedication to leading with love. It's easy to discuss leading with love when times are good, but when you see red ink everywhere you look, maintaining your dedication to lead with love becomes exponentially harder.

After the market collapse of 2008, our park attendance dropped significantly, and we had obligations that would be difficult to meet if the trends got any worse. So I pulled my senior team together and asked, "How can we handle these difficult financial decisions in a way that is consistent with our values?"

Jane, our COO, responded, "We need to identify the overall expense numbers we need to cut and give our local leadership the freedom to achieve it the way they believe is best. We shouldn't decide for them." We all knew that was the right answer.

Soon after, we got most of our park leaders in a room or on the phone, and within thirty-seven minutes, they had made decisions to cut 50 percent of our capital spending plans for the next year. This did not involve job elimination, but investment cuts that would save cash flow and protect jobs in the company.

Fifty percent cuts in less than an hour. That was the most amazing example of leading with love I have ever seen. Everyone understood the urgency of taking action. No one protected their turf or was selfish in their approach. There was complete truthfulness and trust among our team. They responded to what had to be done, and every property contributed. It was a gratifying and timely display of some of the fruits of leading with love.

Love works—not *even* in hard times, but *especially* in hard times.

However, we weren't completely out of the woods. We still needed to locate millions of dollars in further savings, so we reluctantly started talking about a layoff.

"To hit our expense reduction figure," I said, "we'd have to lay off a lot of people. However, we've calculated that if we freeze all wages for a year and if the most senior leaders take a pay cut, we can save about 350 jobs and minimize layoffs." We decided to examine this idea more and talk again in the morning.

The next day, Ken Bell, the president of the Dollywood Company, called me on his way into work. We manage Dollywood for Dolly Parton; it's our biggest property, and it is critical to our success.

"Joel, the entire Dollywood management team wants to take a pay cut. If they do, we can save another fifteen plus jobs.

Stunned, I asked, "All of the management team agreed to this?"

"Yes," Ken said.

Now that's a phone call any leader would love to get! I had only asked my direct reports to take pay cuts, but when Ken's team realized the size of the layoff needed, they used their freedom to decide to get to the number in some other way—by voting to cut their own pay. That's true dedication to leading with love.

Even with the pay cuts, however, our corporate office still had to cut back 10 percent of its workforce to meet the cost reduction target. Instead of terminating people immediately, we gave all of those who would lose their jobs a long notice period in lieu of severance so they could look for a new job while still employed. We also provided counseling services and unlimited time off during work hours for job hunting.

This cost us valuable resources, yes, but our commitment to leading with love meant we understood there was even more value in treating our employees with honesty and kindness.

Our senior leaders were active in helping those who were going to be released find new positions, writing letters of recommendation and making phone calls. We discussed their strengths with potential employers and let them know our reduction in force was driven solely by economics, not performance. As a result, all but one of the people who were going to lose their positions found another job before the notice period ended. The final person had a job within forty-five days of leaving the company.

I don't know what motivates other leaders, but results like that are what get me out of bed in the morning. Where some would fixate on lost revenues or missed goals, we were able to celebrate the continued ability of coworkers we cared about and respected to provide for themselves and their families.

When you lead with love, your definition of success expands, and you will experience more fulfillment at work than you ever dreamed possible — especially when times are tough.

Our team also did a good job of communicating the cutbacks to the entire company. We used multiple forms of communication, including a video message and a letter from me. This is one task I could not delegate, and I explained

- how deep the recession was,
- that we only wanted to cut benefits and head count once,
- each type of cut and the reason for it, and

- that we were going to hold town hall meetings at all our
  properties to further ease our employees through this difficult period.

As a result of how the team handled this communication, our
employee satisfaction scores actually rose in a year when we made
the most difficult decisions in recent history! That was surprising yet welcome evidence that even when forced to take drastic
action, our employees felt involved and informed because we were
leading with love.

As times got harder, we redoubled our efforts to apply some of
the principles of leading with love outlined in this book:

Patient. We were methodical and handled all job-loss discussions with integrity and openness. We took the time
to get input from each property and never rushed to
judgment.

Kind. We encouraged our employees to get through this
together and come out of it a stronger company. We also
encouraged those losing their jobs and actively helped
them look for new work.

Trusting. We treated those being laid off with trust by letting
them stay for six months while looking for a job. All of
them honored that trust, and all of them found jobs.

Unselfish. All the properties made sacrifices, and Dollywood
chose to extend the pay cuts to all managers to save jobs.

Truthful. We were very open in our communication and
didn't mince words. Our employees appreciated hearing
the truth up front.

Forgiving. There was a lot of tension in the midst of tough
discussions. We disagreed, we "fussed and discussed,"
but in the end we made the best decisions we could and
moved forward in a positive way.

Dedication to leading with love isn't just a theory; it's living
out organization-wide processes that identify and measure the

necessary behaviors. It's one thing to *talk* about values like leading with love, but it's another thing to *deliver* on those values, especially in tough times.

That is what dedication is all about.

Leaders who are dedicated to the attributes of love outlined in this book while getting strong financial results will certainly place themselves in a unique but very successful minority in business, government, and the nonprofit world. Dedication is the fuel we need to drive toward our goal: to lead with love today, tomorrow, and forever.

Dedicated
Chapter Summary

☑ Dedicated: stick to your values in all circumstances.

☑ Great leaders need to use both love and power.
- Jesus displayed how to have power but show love.
- Love without power and power without love are ineffective and unhealthy in relationships or organizations.

☑ Great leaders know how to reward people.
- Measure both *be* goals and *do* goals.
- Integrate *be* and *do* goals in your organization's leadership development process.
- Consider a 2 x 2 matrix to evaluate leaders.

☑ Great leaders know how to navigate in tough times.
- It is possible to lead with love in the difficult times, but it takes dedication to the cause.
- Leaders must make difficult decisions; how they handle those decisions separates those who lead with love from those who don't.

10

A CHOICE
YOU MAKE

Be the change you want to see in the
world.

Gandhi

We've made it to the end. I've enjoyed walking through the principles of leading with love, and I hope you have too.

I would like to leave you with this simple thought: *it's up to you*.

Even if your boss or senior leaders don't support leading with love, you can make a difference. You can be a middle manager or factory worker and still make a difference. You can sell cars, park cars, or be an intern and still make a difference.

And despite the lies our culture tries to sell us, isn't making a difference *really* what life is all about? You can live a more fulfilled life at work by being consistent with the values you hold dear in your personal life. True contentment came for me when I consistently acted in alignment with one set of values at work, at home, and in my community. The real power of leading with love is that it unifies your life.

- Do you wonder why more organizations don't lead with love?
- Do you doubt whether you can make a difference in your organization, given its apparent lack of focus on leading with love?
- Do you feel a dichotomy between your personal values and the values you are asked to uphold at work? Do you wish for a deeper connection?

10.1

Leading with Love
When Others Don't

D id you know that fewer than 10 percent of companies today have a clearly defined set of core values and behaviors to which employees are expected to adhere?* In other words, only 10 percent of organizations have *be* goals effectively integrated in their daily practices. Mind you, many organizations write about their mission, vision, and values in their annual report, but that's only lip service unless those *be* goals are integrated into their recruiting, training, evaluating, and promoting. How can an organization claim that its *be* goals are important when none of its leaders' performance evaluations or pay is based on adhering to those values?

The surprising thing is that it has been proven that companies with *be* goals do better financially over time. If you don't believe me, read *Built to Last* by Jim Collins, in which he demonstrates empirically that companies with an unchanging set of core values and behaviors (*be* goals) — while still being open to changes in their day-to-day practices (*do* goals) — outperform those that

---

*Frances Hesselbein and Marshall Goldsmith, eds., *The Leader of the Future 2: Visions, Strategies, and Practices for the New Era* (San Francisco: Jossey-Bass, 2006), 158.

don't have this attribute.* So why do so few organizations have an unchanging set of core values and behaviors?

To begin with, it's *hard* to lead with love. It's much easier to focus only on "hitting the numbers" and not to worry about the impact our actions have on people or how the organization's culture will be impacted by a series of decisions. Worrying about how to implement a set of values and behaviors only seems to get in the way.

For instance, it would be *easier* simply to fire an employee when he misses a budget than it would be to create a plan for improvement and give him another chance. However, *easier* won't build trust in the organization and show others they will get a fair shot too. *Easier* doesn't grow and nurture a strong culture that brings out the best in people, helping them take risks and live without daily fear for their jobs. *Easier* won't build a lasting, healthy organization that attracts the very best and stands the test of time.

Leading with love is a higher testament to one's leadership acumen than simply taking the well-trodden path toward fear-based, power-hungry management. Leading with love demands commitment, strong will, and patience, but the results are second to none.

Are We There Yet?

A second reason organizations don't lead with love is that most leaders mistakenly think profit is an end in and of itself. Consequently, such leaders make profit the focus of all decisions. The problem, however, is that profit doesn't motivate most of the frontline people essential to an organization's day-to-day success.

I was recently asked to speak at an event that also featured Jim Collins — okay, I was more of a warm-up act for the famous author! — but we attended the same speakers' dinner. He and I

---

*Jim Collins and Jerry I. Porras, *Built to Last: Successful Habits of Visionary Companies* (New York: HarperBusiness, 1997), 55.

discussed how great organizations focus on satisfying customer desires while being driven by great institutional cultures—and profits flow secondarily from those primary commitments. Few employees show up every day to work ten- to fourteen-hour days because of corporate profit! Elsewhere Collins has said, "Profitability is a necessary condition for existence and a means to more important ends, but it is not the end in itself for visionary companies. Profit is like oxygen, food, water, and blood for the body; they are not the point of life, but without them, there is no life."* Collins's research and my experience in business both reflect the same truth, that enduring and successful companies are more ideologically driven and less purely profit focused than companies that don't perform as well financially.

The Long Haul

The final reason leading with love is rare is that many leaders simply don't care about the long term. Such leaders demand results today, without regard to the future. Their mind-set is like an investor who buys a house only to flip it for a profit, as contrasted with a wise and visionary buyer who sees a home as a long-term investment *and* a wonderful place in which to raise a family, celebrate holidays, and grow old.

In other words, some leaders couldn't care less what happens to their company after they leave. Is that the kind of organization for which you want to work? Is that the kind of leader you want to be?

Many hedge funds and some private-equity groups work this way. They are interested only in the next three to five years, focusing exclusively on creating an "exit strategy" or "liquidity event" that will enable them to sell the company, realize a big gain on the sale, and leave the company behind. Many times they leave the companies burdened with the results of short-term decisions that

*Ibid.

hurt the long term—often increased debt that may take years to pay back and burden future leaders.

Anyone with half a brain can come into an organization and quickly improve the bottom line by slashing costs, but moves that boost profits in the short term can destroy trust, relationships, and the long-term culture and profitability of an organization. The leader who follows that sort of paradigm often moves on, leaving the organization on life support. We would never approve of parents purchasing expensive toys for themselves or their kids on credit, only to fall into irreversible debt several years later— but we often commend businesses that are run that way.

Sometimes, careers—rather than companies—are essentially built to flip. In larger organizations, many executives move to different divisions or departments every two to three years and make decisions that help short-term results but may hurt the organization for the long term. Similarly, I have seen leaders who have an "on my watch" attitude. If the improvement isn't going to come immediately, under their watch, they don't want to consider it— even though it's clearly the best decision for the organization in the long term.

Leading with love means building organizations that last.

How Will *You* Lead?

Joe Kennedy is a great friend from GM and Harvard Business School and an astute businessman who led Saturn's sales and marketing in the 1990s during Saturn's heyday. Now he's the CEO of Pandora, the skyrocketing Internet-radio startup—a relationship that makes me *slightly* cooler with my kids! He was also a Division I tennis player at Princeton and, not surprisingly, is 147–0 against me on the tennis court over a thirty-year period. Next time we play, and I beat him, I can't wait to say, "Nobody beats me 148 times in a row!"

Joe said something profound about being built to last, and I have never forgotten his words: "There are two essential activities that take time: developing an organization and developing a brand. Those activities are parallel and interdependent. Leadership is about teaching an organization what you stand for; brand building is about teaching millions of consumers what you stand for. Leadership and brand building require time, consistency, and constancy."

Time, consistency, and constancy.

If an organization fails to define its *be* goals, it won't have the necessary consistency in leadership values and expected behavior over time. In other words, the organization won't be built to last. The organization will have no soul, no core beliefs, and those in the organization won't understand or internalize what it stands for. With every new leader, the culture will be different and the employees will be confused. It doesn't take a leadership savant to guess what will happen to that organization over time.

If you have read this far, you know the definition of agape love that can be used at work. You have the tools needed to integrate love into your organization and into your leadership training and evaluation. You understand that companies with strong *be* goals perform better financially than companies that don't. And you also understand why most organizations don't lead with love.

What comes next is up to you: how are you going to lead?

10.2

You Are
Not Alone

If you are reading this book and wish you were a more senior leader so you could have more influence, I have someone you need to meet: Judy Ward. No one at Dollywood has a greater impact on the organizational culture than Judy.

She knows every one of the one thousand plus employees by name—really!

She knows their strengths and weaknesses.

She knows who's doing a good job and who isn't.

She has the ear of all senior leaders at any time.

She excels at her job.

She has a heart the size of Texas, and she always makes sure employees get the support they need through Share It Forward and other programs. Dollywood literally wouldn't be the extremely friendly, successful family entertainment park that it is today without Judy.

And Judy is an executive assistant.

Don't misunderstand me—the job of an executive assistant is a key job that demands extraordinary organizational skills, diligence, intelligence, and a strong work ethic. I know that I couldn't do my job without Jamie, my world-class executive assistant.

Yet no one considers an executive assistant a senior position from an authority standpoint. Typically we cast assistants as "support staff" and look to the "real" leaders in an organization for the "important" decisions and influences.

The Difference One Person Can Make

But consider: Judy is as "senior" as anyone from an influence standpoint, and she has taught me that shaping corporate culture is up to individuals across the hierarchy, no matter what their job title is. Any of us can make a real difference.

Judy works long hours and does whatever it takes to get the job done. She sends emails to the Dollywood team, letting people know about others in the company who need our thoughts and prayers. Her emails serve as a constant reminder that our organization cares about the whole person, not just the numbers they deliver—and that love is our number one leadership principle.

Here is an example of one of her amazing emails. What is instructive is that I literally took the most recent email from Judy—there was no "search for the best" process involved!

Dear Dollywood Family,
Dale Puckett, who has been a member of our Dollywood Family for about 25 years, husband to Mitzi (who works in merchandise), performs with the Kinfolks at our Back Porch Theatre, and is a first cousin to Dolly, passed away yesterday around 1:00 p.m.

I understand that Dale went fishing this past Wednesday and caught his limit. Then on Thursday, he was sitting in his chair playing his guitar when he just went to sleep. Dale left this old world exactly the way he would have wanted to go—quick and playing his guitar!

This goes to show that none of us are promised tomorrow, so we need to hold each other close to our heart and never take anyone for granted, because it may be the last time that we spend with each other. It is always hard to give up someone you love so dearly, so please ask God to touch their broken hearts with His healing touch, surround them with His love so they will never feel alone but will feel His nearness, comfort, and strength....

Thank you all for your love, your prayers, and your support to each other during difficult times. That is what keeps us a close family.

I love you all,
Judy

Never lose an opportunity to bring sunshine into the life of another. A few encouraging words could make a huge difference in someone's life.

Thoughtful and timely emails are only the tip of Judy's iceberg. She stops by to check on those who are sick at home, organizes visits after park hours for those in the hospital, hosts employee reunions for longtime and retired employees, and creates an environment in which all employees feel valued and loved — and in which all employees desire to pitch in to complete whatever task needs to get done to assure we are creating memories worth repeating for our guests.

We try to have a "Judy" at every property. Sometimes it's a human resource manager, an attractions manager, or a health

Michelle (Dollywood employee), with Judy Ward, chief culture champion, and Ramona, park guest.

advocate nurse. At Silver Dollar City, it's June Ward (no relation to Judy Ward), a forty-year employee who runs our chocolate shop and is the "culture cop." Whoever it is, the culture demands that someone take the lead, assuring that the property leads with love for those in need.

Judy and June are living proof that *any* of us can make a huge difference at work. Everyone in an organization is dealing with *something*: problems at home, health issues, financial stress, and whatever else life brings. And everyone needs a leader who leads with love, making them better people and better employees.

The Final Attribute: Humility

Judy and all longtime employees of Herschend Family Entertainment I've met are proof of what a lifetime of leading with love will do to someone: it will make that person *humble*.

In fact, humility is the eighth principle of leading with agape love that HFE leaders are asked to adhere to. Of course, the minute we *try* to be humble we aren't—because we are focused on ourselves, which is why there is no chapter on humility! We become humble only as we focus on others; and if we follow the seven words of love, we will become humble in the process.

Who is the Judy Ward in your organization? Is it you? Or someone who works for you whom you've never acknowledged or enabled?

Remember, *it's up to you*.

10.3

Leading with Love: A Lifestyle

Accepting Jack's offer as related in chapter 1 was the best career decision of my life. Something miraculous happened along the way as I came to work at Herschend Family Entertainment: Jack, Peter, Nelson, and the other leaders taught me something about myself that I needed to learn.

As you know from the story about my father, I grew up without financial means, and I knew early on that I didn't want to have the same financial pressures as my parents. As a result, I always set aggressive goals for myself in all aspects of my life; I was very determined not to follow my father's financial footsteps.

I am not suggesting that my decision was good or right, but I do know that where I came from influenced the career decisions I made. Early in my career, I focused on money and how to get more of it. That's the primary reason we moved ten times in fifteen years. The problem was that my family and I didn't like where I had ended up—as the saying goes, I had climbed the ladder, but it was on the wrong wall.

Life hadn't turned out as I had hoped. I had worked hard, getting straight As in college while playing varsity football and baseball, graduating from Harvard Business School, and then

The house I grew up in. We added an upstairs later, once my dad finally landed his factory job.

climbing the ladder at GM, which had culminated in a rise to the top spot at Saab North America at thirty-six years old.

Yet as I sat in that one-room apartment in California, I was at rock bottom according to the metrics that truly mattered to me. How could I be excited about a work lifestyle that would destroy my family? I didn't know what to do next.

Fortunately, I accepted Jack's offer and learned to lead with love by the example Jack and Peter set. My childhood experiences had influenced my decisions along the way, but it didn't have to determine where I ended up. I needed to quit blaming my financially impoverished upbringing for my unbalanced focus on monetary "success" at all costs and for my unbalanced focus on *do* goals.

In other words, *I* was the problem, not the companies I worked for or the leaders I served. It wasn't their fault I did all I could to succeed at the expense of my family. It wasn't their fault I wasn't more focused on others. It wasn't their fault I had lost my way.

Is that true for you?

Be goals are about defining the kind of people we want to be instead of what we want to accomplish. The great thing about *be* goals is that they are within our control. And, even more importantly, when we live in a manner that is consistent with those goals, we discover contentment and peace such as we have never known before—contentment and peace that we experience independent of the day-to-day numerical imperatives of work.

When I accepted the job at HFE, I simultaneously did something I now encourage you to do: establish personal *be* goals. Since I am a follower of Jesus, mine are based on his words: " 'Love the Lord your God with all your heart and with all your soul and with all your mind.' And ... 'Love your neighbor as yourself' " (Matthew 22:37–39).

So, my *be* goals define how I can love God and love others. My *be* goal definition of "loving others" uses the very same words and principles that I have described in this book, and my focus on loving others in my *personal* life matches perfectly with leading with love in my *professional* life.

This leads to a very important principle: when your personal values match your work values, you stand the best chance of being content. I have had offers to leave HFE, but I have always said no because my personal and professional lives are in alignment, and that contentment is priceless.

Answering the Why Question

Having a single set of *be* goals at home and work provides something even more important than contentment; it gives me an answer to *why*. Why do I get up every day and go to work? Why am I on earth in the first place? What is the meaning of my work? Why does all my toil even matter? These are huge questions—the most important questions we can ask about life. Yet most of us are so busy *with* life we don't take the time to reflect on the depth and seriousness of these questions.

My time at Greenlight.com was a lonely, wilderness experience, but it allowed me to reflect on these "why" questions and to see the relationship between my *be* goals and my *do* goals. Since my *be* goals grow from my faith in Jesus, I came to understand that my *do* goals needed to have the same roots. Jesus gave his followers the ultimate command and challenge: *love others as I have loved you*. In other words, perfectly. The clearest way I know to unify my *do* and *be* goals is to show that God is active in my life at home and at work.

I believe we are created by God to reflect the attributes of love outlined in this book, and this is true whether or not you are a follower of Jesus. After all, being patient, kind, trusting, unselfish, truthful, forgiving, and dedicated doesn't mean you're religious ... it means you're leading with love, and that's how people are wired. We all long for closer relationships in life, and those can only develop when we treat each other with agape love.

None of my *be* goals have *anything* to do with the size of the organization I work for, the prestige of my role, or the income I earn. However, they *do* require my time and energy. When I was traveling more than twenty days per month and working more than seventy hours a week, I had no capacity to love others and nothing left in my tank.

In other words, I was all *do* and no *be*.

I now consider my *be* goals as the top priority in my life. I schedule time to be with my wife (date nights), time to be with my kids (daddy-daughter dates and trips), and time to be with my friends (rounds of golf and accountability calls), and I schedule every day with several leadership issues. Without scheduling these activities and making sure they're a priority, I lack the emotional availability I need to be the husband, dad, friend, and leader I want and need to be.

I have contentment like never before. I am happy with who I am in this season. I am not "searching" for something. I still work hard and am very performance oriented, but I have changed for the better—just ask Marki and our four girls.

What matters to you?

Think carefully about the answer to that question. For me, what matters are the seven principles of agape love that assure, when I am practicing them at work and at home, that I am pursuing what truly matters.

Leading with love is too important to be left to chance. It takes effort to lead with the principles of love—to be patient, kind, trustful, unselfish, truthful, forgiving, and dedicated.

Friend, my final word to you is this: leading with love is worth it. On every level it is more difficult, and on every level it is more rewarding, more fulfilling, more *right* than you can imagine.

Isn't that what you want? Isn't that what you have been longing for all these years? Let's go there together. Let's take a chance and show the world what an organization led by love looks like.

Let's show the world that love works.

A Choice You Make
Chapter Summary

☑ Why don't more organizations and leaders lead with love?
- It's hard. It's easier to just "hit the numbers" without regard to how the decisions impact others.
- It's less about hitting the numbers and more about doing the right thing for the customer and employees over time.
- Great leaders don't build to flip — they build to last.

☑ Everyone matters.
- You can have a strong influence on your organization no matter what position you hold.
- Everyone in your organization is dealing with something. Leading with love will help people get through their struggles.

☑ *Do* versus *be* in all things: model a lifestyle of leading with love.
- *Be* goals are completely within your power to execute.
- Schedule time for your *be* goals just like you do for your *do* goals.
- True contentment comes when we act in alignment with one set of values at work, at home, and in the community.

Appendix
Herschend Family Entertainment History and Properties

Herschend Family Entertainment started in, well, a *cave*. In 1950 Hugo and Mary Herschend leased Marvel Cave near Branson, Missouri. Since they were moving from the bustling city of Chicago to a virtually unheard of place, this was a huge risk.

Hugo was a successful Electrolux salesperson, while Mary was busy raising two young boys, Jack and Peter. They had vacationed at the cave and loved its natural beauty and cavernous "cathedral room." They hoped they could make a living giving people guided tours of this natural wonder.

*The early days—Jack, Mary, and Peter Herschend
at Silver Dollar City (c. 1961).*

So they took the plunge and moved to Branson. The Herschends struggled at first. But soon word traveled about the unique experience visitors enjoyed when they toured the cave. Hugo and Mary and the people they employed were friendly and caring. Customers felt like family. But then tragedy struck: Hugo died unexpectedly of a heart attack, leaving Mary to run the cave with Jack and Peter who were all of twenty and twenty-two years old.

Mary, Jack, and Peter continued to make the cave a special place. They treated customers so well that the lines into the cave became too long. The Herschends built additional paid attractions to entertain guests. Gradually that array of attractions expanded and became known, in 1960, as Silver Dollar City—a theme park that today attracts more than two million guests a year.

Jack and Peter took over managing the park after Mary passed away in 1983 and continued to grow the organization. With the success of Silver Dollar City, the brothers added a water park and an eight-hundred-seat dinner cruise boat in Branson. In 1985 they were invited to become the operating partners for Dolly Parton's Dollywood in Pigeon Forge, Tennessee—a partnership that

*Where it all started—Jack, Sherry, Peter,
and JoDee Herschend at Silver Dollar City.*

would later add Dollywood Splash Country, Dixie Stampede, and Pirates Voyage dinner theaters in three states. In 1998 HFE added Stone Mountain Park in Atlanta to its portfolio of properties.

Looking to diversify, HFE acquired Ride the Ducks, an amphibious tour company, in 2003. Four years later, the company acquired Adventure Aquarium in Camden, New Jersey, and Newport Aquarium in Newport, Kentucky. They also added Wild Adventures, a theme and water park in Valdosta, Georgia, in 2007.

Most recently, in 2011, HFE became the management company for Darien Lake Theme Park Resort in Buffalo, New York, and Elitch Gardens in Denver, Colorado. Both parks feature a theme and water park and are owned by CNL Lifestyle Properties REIT. Today Herschend Family Entertainment properties attract sixteen million guests a year.

Our Locations

A   *Silver Dollar City - Branson, MO* - A spirit of America adventure park with crafts & artisans and live entertainment, rides and festivals.

B   *White Water - Branson, MO* - A tropical themed water attraction and Herschend Family's first water park.

C   *Showboat Branson Belle - Branson, MO* - A 700-seat paddle wheeler that features dining, Broadway-style shows and a beautiful cruise on Table Rock Lake.

D   *Wilderness Campground - Branson, MO* - Pioneer & rustic log cabins, campgrounds & campsites just minutes from nearby attractions in Branson.

E   *Dixie Stampede - Branson, MO - Pigeon Forge, TN* - A Dixie themed dinner show, operated in partnership with Dolly Parton, showcasing live animals, music and entertainment.

F   *Dollywood - Pigeon Forge, TN* - The Smoky Mountain park operated in partnership with Dolly Parton, features thrilling rides, attractions & festivals.

G   *Dollywood's Splash Country - Pigeon Forge, TN* - An Appalachian themed water park and the largest in Tennessee. Operated in partnership with Dolly Parton and voted top 5 best landscaped parks in the world.

(H) **Dollywood Vacations - Pigeon Forge, TN** - *Operated in partnership with Dolly Parton, offering accommodations with exclusive privileges to Dollywood attractions.*

(i) **Stone Mountain Park - Atlanta, GA** - *An entertainment destination and resort featuring the world's largest monolith carving, attractions, a lasershow spectacular and accommodation options ranging from hotel to campground.*

(J) **Evergreen Resort - Atlanta, GA** - *This golf & spa resort provides easy access to attractions and recreation at Stone Mountain Park.*

(K) **Wild Adventures Theme Park - Valdosta, GA** - *A family entertainment destination combining thrill rides, exotic animals, shows, concerts and a water park.*

(L) **Newport Aquarium - Newport, KY** - *A state-of-the-art aquarium with thousands of aquatic creatures, and the only shark ray breeding program in the world.*

(M) **Adventure Aquarium - Camden, NJ** - *A world-class aquarium known for its touch exhibits, underwater hippo viewing area and the most extensive shark collection on the East Coast.*

(N) **Darien Lake Theme Park Resort - Buffalo, New York** - *New York's largest theme park & water park vacation destination, with rides, attractions, a hotel and campground.*

(O) **Elitch Gardens Theme & Water Park - Denver, CO** - *Entertaining guests for more than 120 years, it is America's only downtown area theme & water park.*

(P) **Pirates Voyage - Myrtle Beach, SC** - *A pirate themed dinner show, operated in partnership with Dolly Parton, showcasing live animals, music and entertainment.*

(Q) **Ride the Ducks - Atlanta, GA - Branson, MO - Newport, KY - Philadelphia, PA - San Francisco, CA** - *A fun, informative and engaging land and water adventure aboard an amphibious vehicle.*

Acknowledgments

I would like to thank the following people for their immeasurable contribution to *Love Works*:

Jack and Peter Herschend: For teaching me how to love at work and for being second fathers to me. Your wisdom and humility in transitioning leadership at Herschend Family Entertainment is the greatest example of selflessness I have seen in business. I am humbled almost every day trying to take your legacy forward.

Nelson Schwab: You are the most competent, "on point" leader I have ever worked with, anywhere; yet you remain an earnest and caring man. You are an amazing board chair who has taught me so much about how to lead. I also thank the rest of the HFE board—Chuck Bengochea, Chris Herschend, Rusty Griffin, Todd Schurz, and Donna Tuttle—for your unending support and heady wisdom and advice.

The entire Herschend family, for continuing to support the legacy of leading with love that Jack and Peter built, which demands leadership to balance the tension between people and profits. What a challenge, but also what a blessing.

The senior leadership team at HFE who supported me through this process: Rick Baker, Ken Bell, John Carson, Jane Cooper, Michael Dombrowski, Steve Earnest, Anthony Esparza, Eric Lent, Craig Ross, Brad Thomas, Rick Todd, and Andrew Wexler. Without your contributions to content and your covering me when I couldn't be there, this book would not have been possible.

The thousands of HFE employees who show me how to love every day with the way you treat each other and our guests. Thank you for doing the really hard work of leading with love on the front lines every day.

To the entire team at Zondervan: If there was ever a company that consistently leads from love, it is all of you. From CEO Scott Macdonald to everyone else I have met, I have always felt loved and cared for. Verne Kenney, thanks for believing in me; this would not have happened if not for you. To Cindy Lambert: Your "big picture" editorial insights put the project in the right direction. Thanks for the insightful marketing collaboration of Don Gates, Tom Dean, Madeleine Hart, and Heather Adams, and Jim Ruark for final editing.

Fatima Mehdikarimi: For your enthusiasm, organization, high standards, and lofty goals. You often inspired me when I questioned myself. Most of all, thanks for being willing to tell me the book was off track, even though it was our first meeting. That took guts, and you have what it takes; I am glad I listened. Valerie McCarty, thanks for hiring Fatima and for your early support and inspiration.

Jamie Hawkins: The best executive assistant I have seen, anywhere, who does an amazing job without fanfare or recognition. Your endless work ethic, organization, sense of responsibility, and intelligence allowed me to keep engaged actively in the day to day of HFE while writing the book. I could not have done it without you.

Dale Buss: Thanks for encouraging me to do this, and for being instrumental in getting the initial draft from my cobbled thoughts to the written page. Thanks for your friendship.

Don Jacobson: This project would not have happened without your help and guidance. Thanks for believing in me and for helping me select the right partner in Zondervan.

Sam Horn: For your endless enthusiasm, deep insights, and focus on storytelling; for helping me "find my voice." You are a living and breathing inspiration.

David Jacobsen: You were a Godsend. Your editing insights were invaluable, and you were a thrill to work with. Thank you for making this book so much better.

Vaughn Brock, Dougal Cameron, and Kevin Jenkins: Without your encouragement, I would have never done *Undercover Boss*; and without that, I would have never written this book. Thanks for your lifelong friendship. We are brothers for life.

Marki and our four beautiful daughters—Ryn, Erinn, Jesse, and Anna: For your support and understanding of the endless weekend and late night hours watching me write with my head stuck in a PC, missing too much family time and never complaining about it—even while on family vacations. I love you.

Sincerely,
Joel

Share Your Thoughts

With the Author: Your comments will be forwarded to
the author when you send them to *zauthor@zondervan.com*.

With Zondervan: Submit your review of this book
by writing to *zreview@zondervan.com*.

Free Online Resources at
www.zondervan.com

Zondervan AuthorTracker: Be notified whenever your favorite
authors publish new books, go on tour, or post an update
about what's happening in their lives at www.zondervan.com/
authortracker.

Daily Bible Verses and Devotions: Enrich your life with daily
Bible verses or devotions that help you start every morning
focused on God. Visit www.zondervan.com/newsletters.

Free Email Publications: Sign up for newsletters on Christian
living, academic resources, church ministry, fiction, children's
resources, and more. Visit www.zondervan.com/newsletters.

Zondervan Bible Search: Find and compare Bible passages in
a variety of translations at www.zondervanbiblesearch.com.

Other Benefits: Register to receive online benefits like
coupons and special offers, or to participate in research.

ZONDERVAN®

ZONDERVAN.com/
AUTHORTRACKER
follow your favorite authors